occult

Man's aura is literally a broadcasting station for God's energy and his cosmic rays. Energies of light and the very thoughts of God himself and of the ascended masters combine with the benign thoughts that emerge from the very life plan of the individual and are then beamed or broadcast in all directions into the world of form. Those who are sensitive and can attune with these waves may perceive their nature and their origin, while those who do not understand cosmic law may become beneficiaries of these wondrous energies without ever knowing their source. It makes little difference. We are concerned with overcoming the preponderance of human darkness that is abroad in the world today by literally flooding forth more light through the auras of many souls who shall dedicate their lives as outposts of cosmic regeneration to the planet.

Kuthumi

BOOKS BY THE ASCENDED MASTERS
AND THEIR MESSENGERS

Climb the Highest Mountain

Intermediate Studies of the Human Aura

The Great White Brotherhood
in the Culture, History, and Religion of America

Studies in Alchemy

Intermediate Studies in Alchemy

The Science of the Spoken Word

Vials of the Seven Last Plagues

The Chela and the Path

Cosmic Consciousness
The Putting On of the Garment of the Lord

My Soul Doth Magnify the Lord!

The Greater Way of Freedom

Liberty Proclaims

Quietly Comes the Buddha

Prayer and Meditation

Understanding Yourself

Dossier on the Ascension

Higher Consciousness

Prophecy for the 1980s

Spoken by Elohim

The Mechanization Concept

KUTHUMI
STUDIES OF THE
HUMAN
AURA

Dictated to the Messenger
Mark L. Prophet

Summit University  Press®
Los Angeles

Studies of the Human Aura
A Way of Life Book
Published by
THE SUMMIT LIGHTHOUSE®
for Church Universal and Triumphant®
Box A
Malibu, California 90265

Copyright © 1971, 1975, 1977, 1978, 1980
Church Universal and Triumphant, Inc.

LIBRARY OF CONGRESS CATALOG CARD NUMBER: 74-24022

INTERNATIONAL STANDARD BOOK NUMBER: 0-916766-09-8

Printed in the United States of America
Fifth Printing

Summit University Press®
Los Angeles

Cover design from Michelangelo's *David*.

Contents

The light of the body is the eye: if therefore thine eye be single, thy whole body shall be full of light. But if thine eye be evil, thy whole body shall be full of darkness. If therefore the light that is in thee be darkness, how great is that darkness!

Jesus

Preface

We live in an age when scientists are postulating a "nonphysical matrix," an "electronic blueprint," a "life field" surrounding every living thing on the planet. They call it the L-field, and they say it exists prior to the birth of the physical organism. Researchers have also announced the existence of a thought field or T-field originating in the mind, which in turn controls the L-field. They maintain that this T-field exists independently of the physical brain and that both the T-field and the L-field are influenced by greater electromagnetic fields of the universe.

Such discoveries challenge the very foundations of our conception of life — of our religion, our philosophy and even our science. Where do these fields come from and how are they generated? Did they come forth from a Supreme Being at the dawn of creation? And if so, does this theory suggest a predestination for every cell of life throughout the universe?

In *Studies of the Human Aura,* the Master Kuthumi takes you through areas of knowledge where you will discover a new dimension of yourself and at the same time learn to come to grips with the fast-moving scientific discoveries that are changing the very course of civilization. He demonstrates the principles whereby you can learn the science of perfecting the aura. He explains in concrete terms what scientists are talking about when they speak of the interdependence of all life — the influences of every cell upon every other cell and the interaction of all living things, even with complex galaxies and other systems of worlds.

Kuthumi offers a threefold exercise including visualization, the sealing of the consciousness, and the use of the power of the spoken word in conjunction with meditation. With this exercise you can advance your consciousness, your ability to create, to probe the known and unknown world, and to harness the energy and the intelligence that are native to your soul. This is the knowledge whereby man becomes first the master of his own consciousness and then the master of his world.

If, as the master points out, the aura or L-field is an extension of God, and man by his free will, employing his mind and consciousness, can, as scientists say, impress upon that field his will, then he becomes ipso facto a co-creator with God. This is a fundamental principle of the teachings of Kuthumi—that we have a right to learn the control of the energy within the aura, to intensify that energy, and through the proper use of the crystal flowing stream of the aura to determine exactly what will manifest within our physical forms. Indeed, these instructions on how to use the aura scientifically to lead a healthier and happier life will show you how to implement the startling discoveries that are being made in advanced scientific research.

Studies of the Human Aura successfully weds science and religion as the two pillars in the temple of man's being. All who are concerned with the future of life on this planet, with the balance of our ecology, and with the ultimate destiny of the soul will benefit immeasurably from studying the exciting revelations contained in these twelve chapters, which in themselves anticipate even greater discoveries concerning the electronic blueprint of life. To lead you in the search for the cause behind the effect known as the human aura is the purpose of this work. To show you how to become one with that cause in mind and in energy flow is the aim of the master as he makes contact with the mind and soul of each student of this dynamic course.

Thou Mercy Flame

Mercy is the grace of love,
Forgiveness from above,
Beauteous star-fire might,
Falling rain of light.

Mighty God-caress,
Freedom from distress
Touching mind and heart
With love's divinest part,

Frees the soul from blindness,
Ope's the mind to purest kindness.
Glorious light, enfold all now
In heaven's greenest bough!

Joy of nature's band,
God's extended hand,
Living flame most holy
Answers now the lowly.

No difference does he make—
All his children who will take
His offered cup of love
Perceive his comfort dove.

No darkness in his motive,
But only light and life.
Behold the flaming votive:
We share one common light!

Kuthumi

To Those Who Seek Self-Knowledge

At this point in time and space, humanity are poised on the pinnacle of opportunity. It is an opportunity for enlightenment through self-knowledge, for peace through self-mastery, for freedom through soul awakening, and for harmony and the abundant life through the control of natural forces.

In every age the realization of opportunity is predicated on the wise use of past experience and present potential through self-discipline guarded by the vision of future attainment. The opportunity for enlightenment, peace, freedom, harmony, and the abundant life is a gift of the Creator who has endowed the creation—male and female—with a spark of selfhood, an identity framed in mortality, destined to give way to immortality.

Through the march of the centuries, mankind have pursued one or more aspects of this opportunity to meet a destiny that has inspired poets, writers, artists, scientists, and holy men to envision a better life, a better world, a better race. Mankind have never ceased to be discontent with the present; for somewhere deep within their heart of hearts, they have held the vision of a golden age.

They have dreamed a dream of love—of the science of self-knowledge, of overcoming all ignorance and poverty, and of the lever of truth putting down every form of bondage and despair. And the forerunners of the race, counting not the cost, have never let down their Herculean drive to move mankind toward higher standards and a more fruitful life on earth.

Mankind have always needed teachers to show them how to live in this world and how to prepare for the world to come. And so teachers have come forth — prophets, avatars, Christed ones — carrying the torch of knowledge which they passed to their disciples. Initiates of the laws of cosmos have surrounded the great masters who have appeared on every continent to keep the flame of life on behalf of humanity.

Gautama Buddha, Confucius, and Lao-tzu, Enoch, Elijah, and Melchizedek, Zoroaster, Moses, and Muhammad, Pythagoras, Socrates, Jesus, and Apollonius of Tyana, Bodhidharma, Patanjali, Shankara, Ramakrishna, and the Divine Mother in her many incarnations — each at his point in time and space has guarded the ark of the covenant whereby God has secured for his sons and daughters the science and the art of partaking of the etheric essence of unseen worlds.

Each has inspired souls dwelling in houses of clay to delve into the mysteries of creation, of preexistence and the afterlife, of the music and mathematics of every aspect of being, of pondering the intangible, the unknowable, the ineffable Word by the logic of the mind and the intuitive faculties of the heart. Thus teachers and prophets, messengers and visionaries have pointed the way out of the dilemma of time and space, not failing to reveal the finite as an opportunity to become coordinates of infinity.

Man faced with the dilemma of relativity is not able to realize his opportunity to conquer himself and his world without the word of the enlightened ones. Because they have walked the way of self-mastery in time and space, they can show him how to overcome all conditionings of the human consciousness, all factors of limitation. This accomplished, he can proceed on the cosmic highway to another plane of reality where life is more real, where other sons and daughters of God — unbound by past, present, or future, unburdened by vessels of clay — are working out the challenges of another existence, of cycles beyond our own, of days and nights that we have yet to understand.

God foresaw the moment when humanity would no longer be content to be confined, to be less than divine. God foreknew the hour of the crying-out when the hot coals of man's desiring to be free would burst into an almost uncontrollable flame that would demand that freedom *now.* As if they knew they were gods, mankind assert their independence—breaking the shackles of an iron will, refusing to be bound in slavery, turning over the tables of the moneychangers, challenging any government, any institution, any form of authority whatsoever that would come between the soul and its right to be free here and now.

Yes, God foresaw the day and the hour when humanity would no longer submit to injustice, to ignorance, or to the manipulation of their energies by the fallen ones. And there is a moment in every century—it is a cosmic moment—when at least one soul makes his declaration of independence from every tyrant and every enemy of the flame of freedom. And for every soul who thrusts his mind, his heart, and his will beyond the discord and the din of everyday living, there is a teacher—one who comes forth to point the way, to demonstrate the law, to discipline the awakening consciousness, and to impart the vision of the victory.

The promise of the coming of the messenger of the Lord given to the prophet of Israel is fulfilled in the life of every seeker after self-knowledge whenever and wherever that seeker is willing to submit his ultimate desire for freedom to the discipline of the flame:

"Behold, I will send my messenger, and he shall prepare the way before me: and the Lord whom ye seek shall suddenly come to his temple, even the messenger of the covenant whom ye delight in: behold, he shall come, saith the Lord of hosts. But who may abide the day of his coming? And who shall stand when

he appeareth? For he is like a refiner's fire and like fullers' soap: and he shall sit as a refiner and purifier of silver: and he shall purify the sons of Levi and purge them as gold and silver, that they may offer unto the Lord an offering in righteousness."[1]

There are messengers of the Lord in every plane of consciousness, in every dimension of being. There is the still small voice that speaks to every man, every woman, and every child from deep within the soul. There is the spark of life that beats the heart to the rhythm of God's heart, and there is the mediator who stands, sword in hand, cleaving asunder the real from the unreal, between the human monad and its divine counterpart.

The mediator is the higher consciousness of all mankind — the genius that illumines thought and feeling and action. The mediator is the light that has inspired the great leaders of all time. This is the light that John the Beloved beheld in the Saviour — "the true Light which lighteth every man that cometh into the world."[2] But in some it has burned more brightly than in others. And thus we have identified the light *as* Jesus, *as* Gautama, *as* Enoch, *as* John the Baptist or the Virgin Mary. Although we have seen this light both in and as the person, the light is in fact the eternal *Christos,* the Word made flesh, come again in every son and daughter of God.

In one and all, this light remains the potential for godhood. It is the Christ light that is the mediator between us who are in a state of becoming whole — groping for the true identity of the soul — and the wholeness of our divinity. The mediator mediates on behalf of the soul — between the lower self and the Higher Self — to implement the goal of self-realization through enlightenment, peace, freedom, harmony, and the abundant life.

Only the few in every age have perceived the light

which lighteth every man that cometh into the world and thereby made contact with their own Christ Self. And through that mediator, these few have beheld the Presence of God pulsating in octaves of light and sound whose frequencies are just beyond the plane of Matter, just beyond the scope of the five senses. In this higher dimension that transcends time and space, mankind have a point of contact with infinity. That point of contact is the individualized God Self which Moses beheld in a concentrated focus of sacred fire whence the voice proclaimed the origin of being: "I AM THAT I AM!"[3]

The human self—unrefined, unredeemed—requires the messenger, the mediator whom we call the Christ Self, to prepare the way of the Lord, to make straight the paths of awareness for the coming into consciousness of the law governing all cycles of manifestation. For this law, when practiced, becomes the arc between the human and the divine. The "I AM WHO I AM," who revealed the law to Moses and led the children of Israel over the desert unto the Promised Land, is the I AM Presence, the Flaming One, the sphere of fiery identity out of which is born each individual soul, each individual identity which goes forth in time and space to expand God's awareness of himself. This flaming flame that would not consume nor be consumed is the refiner and purifier of the sons and daughters of God desiring to be free of the encrustations of mortality.

Those who understand that the five senses are limited faculties of perception, capable of penetrating only a limited spectrum of Matter, come inevitably to the realization that the mind and soul of man have the ability to fathom other planes of existence; for these aspects of identity will not be limited to a narrow band that, like two parallel lines, would confine consciousness to a mere compartment of time and space.

Because only the few have probed beyond the finite world to discover an identity and a selfhood beyond the clay vessel, God has sent forth messengers, teachers, and prophets who have stood before them in bodies of flesh and blood. For as John said, the light shone in the darkness and the darkness comprehended it not. But "the Word was made flesh and dwelt among us, and we beheld his glory, the glory as of the Only Begotten of the Father, full of grace and truth."[4]

From century to century, when God desires to make known the presence of the light of the Christ and of the Word as the true messenger of each soul, he sends forth that light veiled in flesh. Until the impersonal light of the Father becomes the personalized light of the Christ in the sons and daughters of God, it is beyond the comprehension of humanity. When humanity can recognize the light as it is personified in the teacher, the prophet, the holy one, then and only then can they acknowledge that light as the light which also kindles the spark of divinity within themselves. Guided by the word and the example of the teacher, they come to recognize that spark as their very own individualized Christ Self who is the eternal messenger of the I AM THAT I AM.

John the Baptist was a messenger for Jesus the Christ. He prepared the way of his coming by preaching in the wilderness of Judea, saying, "Repent ye: for the kingdom of heaven is at hand."[5] His was the voice of one crying in the wilderness of the human consciousness to prepare the way for the descent of the Christ light, the Lord of every soul. As John was a messenger for Jesus the Christ, so Jesus was the messenger for the Christ in every man and woman. Through the ritual of baptism and the confessing of sins, John prepared the minds and hearts of the people to receive Jesus the Christ, who in turn would prepare them to receive their own Christ Self-awareness.

To prepare the consciousness of mankind for the coming of the messengers of the Lord known as the ascended masters is the mission of The Summit Lighthouse and the ministry of Mark and Elizabeth Prophet. The ascended masters are the true teachers of mankind who for thousands of years have served from the planes of Spirit to deliver the teachings of the Christ to humanity. Working through their representatives on earth whom they have anointed as their messengers, the ascended masters have from time to time unveiled the ancient wisdom in both the spoken and the written word.

The Summit Lighthouse was founded in Washington, D.C., in 1958 by El Morya, Chief of the Darjeeling Council of the Great White Brotherhood. Having mastered time and space and ascended into the presence of the I AM THAT I AM, El Morya, together with other ascended masters, has for many years sponsored the release of instruction in the form of *Pearls of Wisdom,* which are weekly letters sent to their chelas on every continent, and Keepers of the Flame Lessons containing fundamental and advanced teachings in cosmic law. The ascended masters have also released numerous books and delivered dictations before large audiences throughout the world.

This instruction has been dictated to Mark and Elizabeth Prophet, who received their training directly from El Morya, Saint Germain, Jesus, Kuthumi, Archangel Michael, and Mother Mary in preparation for their appointment as messengers of the Great White Brotherhood. These revelations are acclaimed by the true disciples of Christ who are willing to listen and to learn of the higher calling of the sons and daughters of God in this age.

The Great White Brotherhood is the organization of sons and daughters of God who have graduated from this system of worlds — who have transcended the domain of Matter and entered into the dominion of the Spirit — and continue to inspire humanity in every walk of life. The Great White Brotherhood has also been called the Inner World Government, inasmuch as it consists of a hierarchy of ascended beings who, when called upon, lend assistance in directing the governments and the economies of the nations and the affairs of all mankind. The Darjeeling Council is a special branch of the Great White Brotherhood dedicated to inspiring the will of God upon heads of state as well as upon all devotees of the very flame which inspired Jesus to pray, "Nevertheless, not my will, but thine be done."[6]

Like John the Baptist of old, the ascended masters are coming to the fore of consciousness and into the arena of action to prepare mankind for the Second Coming of Christ, which is the realization in this historic moment of the Word made flesh in every man, woman, and child upon the planet.

They proclaim the Second Coming of Christ in the appearance of the Christ light in every heart and in the attainment of the Christ consciousness by every soul. They preach the Second Coming as the awareness by each individual of the light potential of the Flaming One within the citadel of being. They say that when all mankind experience this Second Coming, then they will see and behold Jesus the Christ, Mary the Mother, Michael the Archangel, and other messengers of the I AM Presence descending in "the clouds of heaven with power and great glory."[7]

All messengers who have proclaimed the teachings of the ascended masters have done so in fulfillment of the prophecy given to John the Revelator of the empowering of the two witnesses who would "prophesy a thousand two hundred and threescore days clothed in sackcloth."[8] This means that in every

age there are teachers who come forth for a preor-
dained cycle, clothed in garments of mortality, once
again to reveal the light of the Christ that is very real
and present just beyond the flesh and blood of mortals.
With deftness and a one-pointed zeal, every true
teacher marks the perfect man as the Christ in all and
defines each one's contact with the fiery sphere, the
flaming sun center that pulsates behind every son and
daughter of God.

The witnesses are referred to by John as the two
candlesticks.[9] Thus they are always lesser lights giving
forth the glory and the message of the greater light.
Like the torchbearers of ancient Greece who ran in
the torch race in the stadium of Athens, passing the
torch to each succeeding runner, the messengers pass
on the truth that has descended from the Ancient of
Days[10] to a new generation of souls who have determined to be free. The "God of the earth" before
whom they stand is the Lord of the World, Gautama
Buddha, another messenger of the light of far-off worlds.

Lord Gautama, a messenger in the plane of
Spirit, anchors his consciousness of God in the
threefold flame of life that burns on the altar of
Shamballa, an inner retreat of the Great White
Brotherhood — a point of infinity anchored in etheric
dimensions corresponding with the Gobi Desert in
Central Asia. Thus Gautama is a messenger for beings
whose awareness of God is beyond his own, beings who
form a chain of hierarchy, like the golden chain of
Hermes, that moves from this point in time and space
all the way back to the nucleus of our cosmos called the
great central sun.

Serving under this "God of the earth" are other
hierarchs who release the messages of the masters to
those among mankind who have recognized the
requirements of self-knowledge, self-mastery, and the
control of the forces of nature in order that they might

fulfill the cycles of opportunity at hand and be free from the rounds of mortality.

Directly under Gautama Buddha is Maitreya, who keeps the flame of the Cosmic Christ on behalf of earth's evolutions. He is known as the Great Initiator, for he initiates the souls of mankind in the exercise of the laws of harmony according to the tradition of the teachers and avatars of all ages. His disciplines are for those who are willing to sacrifice the human ego, the human will, and the human intellect, that they might become the fullness of the presence of the Christ which Jesus was. Lord Maitreya is responsible for releasing the wisdom of the Buddha through the heart, head, and hand of the Divine Mother as she teaches the children of the Father the ways of righteousness and truth.

Those who would approach the guru Maitreya must be prepared for the ultimate tests of the cross and of the sacred fire as well as the disciplines that are necessary to prepare the soul for those tests. Jesus served under this hierarch during his Galilean ministry; and his discipline of fasting forty days in the wilderness was given to him by Maitreya to prepare his consciousness for the three tests of the carnal mind personified in Satan.[11]

First was the test of love wherein Jesus was tempted to use his alchemical powers to command "these stones be made bread." He passed the test by affirming that man does not live by bread alone but "by every word that proceedeth out of the mouth of God."

Second was the test of wisdom wherein the Christed one was challenged to tempt the Lord God by casting himself down from the pinnacle of the temple. He put down this temptation by refusing to wrest the meaning of the scriptures which the devil quoted to him ("He shall give his angels charge concerning thee: and in their hands they shall bear thee up, lest at any time thou dash thy foot against a stone").

Third was the test of power wherein the initiate was taken up into a high mountain and shown the glory of the kingdoms of the world and offered "all these things" if he would fall down (lower the frequency of his mind, debase the energies of being) and worship the evil one. With a final command, Jesus passed this threefold test: "Get thee hence, Satan: for it is written, Thou shalt worship the Lord thy God, and him only shalt thou serve."

Because Jesus passed the tests of the Great Initiator at every hand—proving the victory of life over every form of limitation, including sin, disease, and death—he was taken through the advanced initiations of the transfiguration, the crucifixion, the resurrection, and the ascension. In each successive initiation, body, soul, and mind became more and more filled with the light of the Christ until "the fashion of his countenance was altered, and his raiment was white and glistering."[12]

In the initiation of the crucifixion, Jesus willingly laid down his life to prove the immortality of the soul and the power of the resurrection flame to restore the action of body, soul, and consciousness in Matter. Forty days after the fulfillment of the resurrection spiral within him, he passed from a point in time and space, a point of opportunity, into that point of infinity which he recognized as the I AM Presence—the Sun behind the Son, the Divine Monad itself.

Today, from that point in infinity, Jesus the Christ continues to serve mankind as a messenger of the light in the office of World Teacher. Sharing that office with him is another devotee of the Lord, one called Kuthumi, who also walked the earth in the role of teacher and sage. Together they serve under Lord Maitreya to bring the wisdom of the ages to mankind in this their hour of opportunity to become initiates of the sacred fire.

The World Teachers have sponsored the education of souls in the Christ light at every level from
preschool through primary and secondary education to
college and university levels. In every nation on earth,
they have inspired teachers, philosophers, scientists,
artists, professional and nonprofessional people with
the wisdom of the ages as it applies to each particular
culture, even as the many cultures of the world serve to
bring forth the many facets of the Christ consciousness.

Currently the World Teachers are delivering to
the disciples of Christ and of the Buddha the instructions of the hierarchy concerning the method and the
mode of self-knowledge, self-mastery, aspects of soul
awakening, and the control of natural forces. This
they are accomplishing not only through publications
and conferences of The Summit Lighthouse, but also
in a thorough and ongoing program of studies being
offered at the ascended masters' university in Los
Angeles, California. Under the sponsorship of Lord
Gautama, Summit University was founded by the
Prophets in July 1971 as an outer arm of the Great
White Brotherhood, an intermediary at the organi-
zational level between humanity and the hierarchy
of ascended masters.

On February 26, 1973, Mark took his leave of this
octave, as he said he would, passing through the ritual
of the ascension. Today he is affectionately called
Lanello by his students, young and old, as he continues
to guide their progress on the path and that of the
organization as well. In addition to teaching the
law and counseling students at Summit University,
lecturing, and supervising the publishing of the
masters' teachings, Elizabeth serves in the role of
Mother of the Flame, a spiritual office designated by
hierarchy for the one who serves directly under the
World Mother to nourish the flame of life on behalf of
earth's evolutions.

Since the World Teachers have come to the fore in this decade to give dispensations of knowledge, of the correct use of the sacred fire, of the laws of alchemy and the understanding of karma and re-embodiment, it is an auspicious moment for the release of *Studies of the Human Aura* by the Ascended Master Kuthumi. A series of twelve letters dictated to Mark L. Prophet, these writings are directed to all who count themselves disciples of Christ, chelas of the masters, seekers after the ancient wisdom.

The Master Kuthumi is the head of the Order of the Brothers of the Golden Robe, a fraternity composed of ascended masters and their embodied chelas dedicated to the enlightenment of all mankind through the wisdom ray. His retreat is in the etheric dimension corresponding with Kashmir, India. He also maintains a focus at Shigatse in Tibet. Kuthumi is known to students of theosophy as the Master K.H., who, together with the Master El Morya, founded the Theosophical Society through H.P. Blavatsky in 1875. The purpose of their outreach in that endeavor was to acquaint mankind with the hierarchy, the ascended masters, the path of initiation, and the wisdom of the ages that underlies all of the world's religions and comes down to us through the mystery schools which have guarded the science of the soul since the last days of Lemuria and Atlantis.

Studies of the Human Aura represents the continuation of the work begun by the Master K.H. shortly before he passed through the initiation of the ascension in the latter nineteenth century. Since then, Kuthumi has tended the golden flame of illumination upon the altar of his retreat with the absolute conviction that one day all mankind would respond to its pulsations through their own inner attunement with that mind which was in Christ Jesus. In his embodiment as Pythagoras, Kuthumi acknowledged the flame as the focal point of his school at Crotona. As Saint Francis, he worshiped the Christ and sought to walk in the footsteps of his Master as he assumed the identity of the divine poverello.

As Jesus before him had said, "Heaven and earth shall pass away, but my words shall not pass away,"[13] so the Master K.H., in his final incarnation in India, expressed his supreme confidence in the immortality of divine knowledge, even as that knowledge makes its way in the marts of the world—taken up by some, cast aside by others. Writing to his disciple A. O. Hume, the master said:

"Fear not; . . . our knowledge will not pass away from the sight of man. It is the 'gift of the gods' and the most precious relic of all. The keepers of the sacred Light did not safely cross so many ages but to find themselves wrecked on the rocks of modern scepticism. Our pilots are too experienced sailors to allow us [to] fear any such disaster. We will always find volunteers to replace the tired sentries, and the world, bad as it is in its present state of transitory period, can yet furnish us with a few men now and then."[14]

It is our prayer that in publishing these letters, we can yet furnish the World Teachers with a few men and women in this age who will seize the torch of knowledge and carry it far and wide to reach the children of God—the many who are waiting for the fulfillment of the promise of the coming of the messenger of the Lord.

I

The Perfecting of the Aura

To All Who Would See and Know and Be the Truth:

As we commence these auric studies, let it be understood that the combined manifestation of body, soul, and mind creates around the spinal column and the medulla oblongata those emanations called by some the human aura and by others the magnetic forcefield of the body of man. Let it be understood by all who read that each individual in whom is the flame of life reveals himself as though he were to shout it from the housetops — all that he really is, all that he has done, and even the portent of that which he shall be — right in the forcefield of his being and in the magnetic emanations surrounding his physical form.

The reading in depth of the human aura is no ordinary science. Those who would undertake to do so should understand that by a simple change in thought the fountain of the human aura, which pours forth from its own orifice, can change its color, its emanation, its magnetic affinity — its complete identity; yet at the same time it may retain beneath the surface the capacities to poison the atmosphere of the individual or the auric emanation within, by virtue of his failure to cleanse himself in heart.

"Blessed are the pure in heart: for they shall see God"[1] is more than a beatitude issuing from the mouth of the living Christ. It is a fiat of strength shining, promised to all who behold it. We have pondered the great need of humanity for purification, and we advocate above all the purification of motive. But when individuals do not see clearly just what their own motives are, it becomes exceedingly difficult, by reason of their own internal blindness, for them to purify themselves.

Therefore, the purification of the faculty of vision has been given top priority by the masters, because it has been our experience that when men learn to see as God sees, they perceive the need to correct their problems and in most cases do so without further delay. In the matter of our Brotherhood, those unascended devotees who wear the golden robe of cosmic illumination, who in truth are illumined concerning the many subjects ordinarily hidden from the average seeker on the path, are expected to perform more advantageously in directing their lives according to the instructions issuing from their lips. A good example is the best teacher.

Now, what is the object of humanity's desire to read the human aura? Is it simply to satisfy some quality of human curiosity, or do they find satisfaction in perceiving the wrongs of others without correcting their own?

All who undertake this study of auric emanations and of the human forcefield as it pours forth into space should recognize the creative nature already existing in mankind. By the misuse of the creative nature, men have fabricated in countless lives undesirable and unwholesome conditions which plague their young, disturb their elders, and in no way contribute to the growth of the quality of human life as originally envisioned by Almighty God.

The hope of the world as the light of the world is to be considered. The world today emanates an aura not at all resembling the Christic aura of the universal Christ consciousness; and the bulk of the people remain in ignorance of the simplest cosmic truths because the powers of darkness that are in the world have accomplished the distortions of the Scriptures which they desired long, long ago. Man's interpretation of his relationship to the Divine involves itself in pagan, anthropomorphic concepts. God is seen as being appeased by sacrifice; even so, men fail to understand the true meaning of sacrifice.

In the case of the Master Jesus, because of the perfection in his nature, which he clearly perceived, he did not require any propitiation for sin; yet he is portrayed as one who is able to save to the uttermost those who believe in him. Those who understand the meaning of God, Christ, and life from a real standpoint see that there is no difference between the divine nature in Jesus and the divine nature in themselves. They understand that there is no partiality in heaven. All can equate with the image of the beloved Son. The ninety and nine must be forsaken,[2] for they already possess the strength within themselves to perceive this truth. And the one who is lost, caught in the brambles of confusion, blinded to his own reality and the inward radiance of the divine image, must now forsake the false doctrine of the blind leaders of his blindness; he must heed the voice of God and return to it.

Through our auric studies which we are releasing herewith, we anticipate that many shall find their way back to the Father's house. There they will perceive that they must present themselves a living sacrifice unto God. It was never the Father's intent to collect penance from humanity nor to exact a form of sacrifice as appeasement of his wrath; for the only

wrath of God that is valid in the cosmic courts of
heaven is that karmic recompense, that weight of sin
which imputes to humanity the darkness they have
created, acceded to, or acknowledged.

In reality man lives in a universe of light and
purpose. To veil that purpose from man was never the
intention of God; for he has clearly said, "That which
has been hidden shall be revealed."[3] In this sense,
then—the higher sense of releasing the divine knowing
within man, who in reality is both the knower and the
known—do we finally establish the reality of God
within the consciousness of the individual, thus pro-
ducing right there in man the perfection that he
craves.

It is amazing how by ignorance men are thwarted
in their attempts to understand life. Simply because
they do not know, they do not find out. Therefore, as
our beloved Master once said, "For whosoever hath, to
him shall be given and he shall have more abundance:
but whosoever hath not, from him shall be taken away
even that he hath."[4] He spoke of understanding. This
most precious treasure we shall attempt to bequeath to
you in our releases on the *Studies of the Human Aura.*
All who read should bear in mind that we cannot
increase the knowledge of those who do not first invoke
it from the throne of grace.

It is of utmost importance that the student understand that there is a process whereby every observa-
tion of his five senses is transmitted automatically
to subconscious levels within himself where, by inner
hieroglyph, events he has witnessed or matters which
he has studied are recorded; thus the entire transmittal
of data from the external world to the internal lies in
the akashic records[5] of his own being. The process of
recall, while quite involved from a technical standpoint, is almost instantaneous. Out of the storehouse of
memory, man quite easily calls forth these treasures of

being. Unfortunately, not all events are benign; not all recordings are examples of perfection.

The sorting and classification of these records is the responsibility of the body elemental and the recording angel of the individual lifestream. You will find mention of the recording angels in the words of Jesus when he spoke of the little ones, "For I say unto you that their angels do always behold the face of my Father which is in heaven."[6] Each individual has such an angel representing the purity of the infinite God, assigned to his lifestream by divine decree from the very foundation of the world. This angel has not only the ability to read the life record of everyone upon the planet, but also to commune directly with the heart of God, "to behold the face of my Father which is in heaven." Thus the intent of God to reveal himself unto the angel of his Presence, attached to each of his children, operates through the Holy Christ Self in perfect harmony with the divine plan.

How unfortunate are those who, while always perceiving the height and depth of man, are never able to become impersonal enough in their approach to endow "the least of these my brethren"[7] with the quality of the living Christ. Men find it not at all difficult to believe that the fullness of the Godhead bodily dwelleth in Jesus,[8] but they do find it difficult to believe that it also dwelleth in themselves. Yet this God has done. He has in the bestowal of the Christ flame placed the fullness of himself in every son and daughter. When the divine nature is properly understood then, how easily humanity can bring forth the *antahkarana*[9] and thus begin the process of correctly weaving their life manifestation.

Now, as man studies the science of perfecting the aura, he should also understand that through the misqualification of thought and feeling, many undesirable traits are brought into manifestation. Most

dangerous of all is misqualification in the emotional
body of man, in the feeling world; for thereby the
heart is touched and in turn often sways the whole life
record of the individual into a miasma of doubt and
questioning.

I do not say that the sincere student does not have
the right to question or even to doubt; but I do say that
once the truth is clearly presented to him, if the door
of his heart be open, he will never doubt and never
question the truth of the living God. He may not leap
over the hurdle; but he will clearly perceive that it can
truly be, that he will be able, yea, that he *is* able to
realize more of God than that which his present
awareness allows. Let us free humanity by right
knowledge from all that has bound them and blinded
them to their own great inner power, to the treasure-
house God has locked within their consciousness.

Now I want to make very certain that all understand that misqualification in the feeling world—such
as anger, self-righteousness, fear, hatred, jealousy,
condemnation, and resentment—gives a certain lever-
age to the power of amplification. This is similar
to the transponder system on your large aircraft. When
the transponder button is pushed by the pilot, it
triggers a signal from the transponder which causes an
enlarged blip to appear upon the electronic board of
the airport traffic controller, thereby enabling the
plane to be easily identified. Thus do the emotions of
mankind often falsely amplify misqualified thoughts
and feelings to the point where a dominant position is
assumed by these misqualified feelings. Although this
takes place without the consent of the real being of
man, nevertheless, darkness does, then, cover the
earth. Yet Christ has said, "I AM the light of the
world."[10]

I have given you many thoughts in this my first
release on *Studies of the Human Aura*. The Brothers

of the Golden Robe will joyously respond to the depth of his wisdom which we shall release in the completed series. From the archives of the Brotherhood our love pours forth.

Devotedly,

Kuthumi

II

The Susceptibility of the Aura

To Every Chela Who Seeks the Light of the World:

Continuing auric studies, we examine the influences of the world upon the human monad. Man is a creature of simple design, yet complex in the externalization of that design. Little do men realize, when first they ponder the nature of themselves, the ramifications of the consciousness of each individual. The influences of the world, the thoughts of the world, the feelings of humanity are easily transmitted consciously or unconsciously from person to person; and in the transmittal of thoughts and feelings, neither sender nor receiver has any guarantee that the patterns of his intent will be preserved intact.

If the light that is in man that he transmits is undesirable,[1] those who are easily made the victim of his thoughts and feelings or those who are naturally affinitized with him may reproduce the effects of those thoughts and feelings in their own worlds. So many in the world today are victims of the thoughts of others — even thoughts from other eras, which endure because mankind have fed their attention and their energies into them.

In effect, it can be said that man has endowed either his evil or his good deeds with a semipermanent existence, and that the consciousness of good and evil partaken of by Adam and Eve, because it has been perpetuated by his free will, is living in man today. Yet, through a return to the Edenic consciousness of God, man is able to find the tree of life, which is in the midst thereof, and to eat of the fruit and live forever.[2]

There is much that we shall transmit in our studies, but first we must ask that the students approach them with the right attitude in order that we may create a climate of the practical use of right knowledge. Through the ages that have passed from spiritual innocence to worldly contamination, men have seldom observed the recycling process by which there has been regurgitated upon the screen of life a flood of undesirable qualities. Both world and individual problems have been prolonged entirely because of the vibrational patine of blackened and tarry substance with which man has coated his very being and then refused to surrender.

It is time humanity began to examine themselves as individuals having a creative potential which they may use to influence the auras of others and which in turn makes them susceptible to influences from others, both good and bad. Thoughts of love, joy, and peace — divine thoughts created in the hearts of the saints and the angelic hosts — should never be avoided, but should be enhanced by the magnetic forcefield of the aura. Men can learn from one another, and their auric emanations can benefit from contact with those whose auras are filled with virtue.

Because it is just as easy for the aura to absorb vice as it is for it to absorb virtue, the individual must understand how this process of thought and feeling transmittal can help or hinder him in his daily occupation. Because people are so completely unaware of the effects of the mass consciousness, as well as the mental pressures from neighbors and friends, we continue to stress the importance of using the violet transmuting flame and the tube of light as effective deterrents to the penetration of the aura by undesirable qualities and to their effects upon the mind and being.

Needless to say, I am determined to transmit in this series definite information that shall make it easier for the soul within man to hold dominion over his life pattern, thus improving the quality of the human aura. Unless this be done, great pain and suffering will undoubtedly come to humanity, and that unnecessarily. The Brothers of the Golden Robe, in their devotions and study of the holy wisdom of God, have recently considered that a clearer revelation of matters involving the human aura would make it possible for more individuals who are oriented around spiritual knowledge to be assisted and to assist others; hence this series.

Now, without question there are problems manifesting in the world wholly as a result of the individual's contact with the auric field or forcefield of embodied humanity. Therefore, defenses must be clearly shown. They must be understood at the level of the individual. In addition to that, methods of projecting the consciousness or the forcefield out of the physical body and to others in one's immediate family or circle of friends must be understood and then effectively mastered as a means of sending hopeful light rays of cosmic service to those who, while in need of assistance, have no idea whatsoever that such possibilities exist.

Although people are brought under the benign or harmful power of various auric manifestations and forcefields, they do not understand how this is done; and many times they are unaware that it is being done.

It is not a question of scientific marvel to them or one of strange phenomena — they simply do not know that it exists. But we do. Working effectively with this knowledge from a wholly constructive standpoint, the angelic hosts and Brothers of the Golden Robe yearn to see the day manifest when humanity, one and all, will understand how they may use this beneficent force of the human aura in a correct and proper manner. For they will see that the aura is designed to be a reflector of Good to all whom they meet and to the world at large.

Those skilled in mortal hypnotism and seductive practices have a partial knowledge of the use of auric and forcefield projections; and they do achieve limited results that lend credence to their work in the minds of some whose goals are likewise limited. As our beloved Master Jesus once said, "The children of this world are in their generation wiser than the children of light."[3] In conference with us, beloved Jesus has made very clear that in making that statement it was never his intention to see this condition prevail. Rather it was his promise to all who believed in the Christ, "Greater works shall ye do because I go unto my Father."[4]

Thus it is the will of God that each generation should attempt to improve the quality of the abundant life upon the planetary body through every available means that is in keeping with the teaching and practice of the Christ.

It has been our intent in these first two releases to give certain vital bits of information on our subject. Later in the series we shall develop that understanding of our instruction which, if correctly applied, can change your life and the lives of countless numbers among mankind because they will be better able to appreciate and to follow the way of truth and the way of hope.

Do you know how many individuals there are in

the world today who by reason of their ignorance on these very subjects become the victims of the manipulators? Well, beloved ones, there are many, I assure you. And I do not want the graduates from our class to ever again be among them.

Let me then go back to the basic principles of ascended-master law by citing for all the need to use your tube of light and the violet transmuting flame as the greatest protection you can ever have against the forces of manipulation. How very dominant, God-endowed, and beautiful are the fragments of divine knowledge that have been received by you thus far.[5] Do you truly meditate upon them? Do you make them a part of your life? Or do you find them to be entertaining flowers that somehow the mind takes a fancy to?

Beloved ones, I want to prepare you for a most tremendous piece of information which I will transmit to you in a forthcoming lesson. But I want to make certain that when you receive this concept which I will bring to you, you meditate upon it like a flower. I give you a full week from this *Pearl of Wisdom* to the next to prepare yourselves in your meditations for this concept, which I assure you will give you a very concrete idea beyond the mechanical as to just how you can accomplish the purification of your aura. Without this knowledge that I am about to reveal, a great deal more time could very well elapse before you would truly understand the real freedom you have and how to use it for the blessing of all life.

When you divinely apply the wisdom of the Great White Brotherhood to the correct manifestation of reality in your world, I am certain that the improvement in your aura and in the quality of your life will be very great indeed. Remember that I want you to be a flower—a rose or a lotus—waiting in the swamplands of life to receive the precious drops of

truth that heaven has prepared for you. If you will do
this, I am certain that you will need no further proof of
the reality of your being, of the unfolding kingdom
that is within you, and of how you can take dominion
over that kingdom, as God intended, in a way that is
safe, sane, and correct.

When there are so many books being written
today, so many words being released into the stream of
mankind's consciousness which are almost a complete
abortion of the divine intent, I must urge you to
appreciate the opportunity we are releasing to you
today.

Devoted to your heart's light,
I remain

Kuthumi

III

The Colorations of the Aura

To the Keepers of the Light in Every Age:

The reality of your God-perfection, latent in all life, is continually releasing the current of its magnificence into your consciousness. Whenever an impediment blocks the flow of this magnificent God-energy, it is as though an object has opaqued the light of the sun. As the sun has its corona, so there is always a spillover of the delightful radiance of the vital life forces in man, which are so easily subjected to his negative influences and misuse. This discolors the aura with negative vibrations and leads man to draw the conclusion that he is less than the perfection of God.

Just as men recall on a cloudy day that the radiance of the sun is behind the clouds and can be seen from an aircraft which penetrates the clouds, so man should also begin to develop and maintain the habit of constantly telling himself that the blazing, dazzling reality of the fullness of God is being released to him moment by moment as the master plan of eternal purpose. Thus he should develop the habit of counteracting all examples of shadow and misqualification by applying the principle of internal reality.

What is real? What is real is released to man as he practices the ritual of penetration — of penetrating the light of the Son of God by the very power of the light that is within him — and thereby more and more of the divine radiance can infuse the aura in its manifest pattern. Therefore, today the delight of the law of God will be in the mouth of the man or woman who will speak the living Word,[1] invoking from the heart of God that magnificence which he already is, claiming in the Word, I AM, the fullness of the Godhead bodily in himself[2] as a joint heir with the universal Christ consciousness.[3]

Now, in the matter of the effects of one's thoughts and feelings upon the human aura, we shall briefly touch upon the subject of coloration. As the intensity of the white and the violet light is increased in the aura, especially those shades which are pale and ethereal, one notes the enlarging of man's perceptions and an increase in spirituality. As the pale yellow — almost golden — light floods through the mind, the very fingers of cosmic intelligence manifest as interconnecting light rays, enabling the mind of man to contact the universal mind of God.

By amplifying in the aura the beauty of pastel pink — vibrating fire of the cup of universal love — man is able to spill over into the world the very thoughts of divine love. As so many know, the color of violet, vibrating at the top of the spectrum, is transmutative and buoyant. Born to the purple, the man who so infuses his aura is cloaked in the invincibility of the King of Kings. This royal color is the cosmic fire of the Holy Spirit which, when blended with the azure blue of the will of God, manifests as divine love in action in that holy will. The green light, eternally new with abundance, charges the aura of man with the power of universal healing and supply. To seal all in the will of God is to drink from the goblet of that holy will. In the electric blue of the ascended masters, it denotes both purity and power.

Now, not all of mankind see the aura, and for some it is perhaps a misstatement to say that they do. What happens in most cases is a sensing, by the inner being of the reader, of the auric emanations of others and the interpolation thereof by the mind through the organ of vision. The impressions of the impinging aura carried over the nerve pathway as a result of the extension of the reader's consciousness into the domain of the magnetic emanation, seem themselves to be seen, when in reality they are only felt. Vibrations of anger often register as crimson flashes, just as black is seen in the aura as the opaquing by negative thoughts and feelings of the otherwise natural release of the light of the Presence through the being of man.

Remember, beloved ones, that the tone of the divine aura is an extension of God, just as the mode of thinking and feeling is the extension of the human consciousness. The interference with the aura in its natural, pure state by the mortal consciousness and its misqualification of light create the negative colorations that are both seen and felt by the more sensitive among mankind. The muddying of the pure colors of the aura occurs whenever there is a mingling of the emanations of imperfect thoughts and feelings with the pure colors released through the prism of the Christ. This marked change in color and vibration is obvious to the trained eye.

In this connection, may I say that one can learn to discern the thoughts and feelings of mortal men and to perceive what is acting in their world. The difference between momentary passions, consciously willed, and sustained deep-seated emotional trends must be considered. How easy it is to see through the process of auric discernment that which is not immaculate in someone's feelings, thoughts, or acts without under-

standing that only a temporary surface disturbance
may have taken place. Much later, if that one is not
careful to override such disturbances by retraining the
mind and feelings and consciously governing the energy flow, an in-depth penetration may occur whereby
auric contamination will reach subconscious levels and
thus prolong the time span of man's indulgence in
negative states.

Great care should be exercised by all who desire to
amplify the immaculate God-concept of others to see
that they do not, by their incomplete perceptions,
actually intensify those negative conditions which those
whom they would assist may not be harboring at all,
but are only entertaining momentarily. Then, too,
there is the matter of the projection of mass forcefields of negatively qualified energy which can become
a patine, or layer of substance, overlaid upon the
natural vibration of individuals. Although totally
foreign to their forcefield, this overlay of darkness, if
seen at an inopportune moment, may be diagnosed by
the careless or untrained observer as an outcropping of
the bedrock of his identity.

Always remember, dear hearts, that those who
fall in the swamp may come up covered with mud; for
the quicksands of life, by their very nature, always seek
to drag man down. But man can and does escape these
conditions, overcoming through the same glorious
victory that brings forth the lotus in the swamplands of
life. I want you to understand, then, that by a simple
act of invoking the light of the Christ consciousness,
man can overcome the ugly chartreuse green of
jealousy and resentment, the muddied yellow of selfish
intellectualism, the crimson reds of passion, and even
the almost violet black of attempts of self-righteous
justification.

To see others clearly, beloved hearts, remember
that man must first perceive in himself the beautiful

crystal of cosmic purity. Then, casting the beam out of his own eye, he can see clearly to take the mote out of his brother's eye.[4] By the purification of your perceptions, you will be able to enjoy the entire process of beholding the Christ in self and others, as one by one the little disturbances of the aura are cleared up through the natural manifestation of the childlike beauty of cosmic innocence.

What is innocence but the inner sense? And the poem of victory that God writes through man is already there in matrix and in creative form, waiting to be delivered upon the pages of life. Human density may have interfered with the manifestation of the Christ in man; but the light and love of the law will produce for him the greatest purification, making possible the penetration of the aura by the beautiful colors of the Christ consciousness.

I should like our students throughout the world to join with me this week in a determined effort to let the crystal-clear grace of the throne which is within you as the threefold flame (three-in-one, hence *throne*) ray out into your world such ecstatic, electrical cosmic energy that you will literally vaporize the darkened elements of your own aura and hence develop that magnificent seeing that will bring the joy of the angels and the light of God to all whom you meet.

Perhaps we shall become more technical, but I think in no way can we become more practical than we have in that which I have already spoken.

Will you follow the Christ of your being in this regeneration?

Devotedly,

Kuthumi

IV

The Reading of the Aura

To the Pupil in Search of a Teacher:
    The trials of life that come to man are in reality his teachers, that is to say, they substitute for his teachers because he will not hear them; yet it has been clearly recorded in the Scriptures and ancient writings that the time would come when man should see his teachers and that they should not be far removed from him.[1]
    So many today are concerned with the facial expressions and appearances of the teachers without ever realizing the lines of character and soul reality that comprise the inner being of a man or woman. Let the true seekers be concerned, then, not so much with the outer beauty of appearances, but with the inner beauty that produces those manifestations in the human aura which bring the admiration of every ascended master because they are the fulfillment of the God-design.
    If any of you have ever been judges in a contest of beauty, you will understand the difficulty in making a selection from among the manifold aspects of God's beauty. In the case of the ascended masters and

Karmic Lords, it is sheer delight that motivates them to pronounce their seal of approval on all that is the God-intent in those who aspire to represent the Brotherhood and to glorify God in their body and in their spirit.[2] And what a marvelous forte of possibility exists for every man! I want our students to think of the richness of the natural, radiating, consecrating devotion that God has placed within man. The opportunity to express the perfection of the Holy Spirit, when rightly apprehended, enables man to fashion the wedding garment of his very Christed being.

Now, I know that through the years many of the students of the occult have stressed the ability of the advanced disciple to read the human aura, to interpret it, and, in effect, to see it. May I say at this time, and quite frankly so, that no psychic ability or even the ability to read the human aura denotes in the person who does so, that mastery by which the true adept overcomes outer conditions.

I do not say that adepts do not have this ability. I simply say that the possessing of this ability, in partial or even in total proficiency, is not necessarily an indication of the advanced spiritual development of the individual. Also, it should be realized that those who profess to read the human aura may do so very poorly, in a confused manner, or in a very limited depth. In order to correctly interpret the reading of the human aura, one must be able to read the karmic record and to have some insight into the total being of a man.

I would far prefer that the students would consider the benefit that can come to them through beholding good in themselves and in others and through striving for the good, as my beloved cohort El Morya has said. For the fruit of striving may not always be apparent on the surface, even on the surface of the aura; but it stands behind the real life record of man's attainment. This is why God has said, "Judge not, that ye be not judged."[3]

Here at Shigatse we concentrate on the sending-forth of holy wisdom; we concentrate on harmony and on true loveliness. There are times, of course, when man must perceive that what is acting in his world is not of the Christ. It is then that he must be able to disentangle himself from his problems and to recognize that neither his problems nor the unwholesome conditions that surround him are the nature of God. Therefore, the Lord does not require him either to prolong his problems or to be weighted down by his environment. Might I add that by nurturing the divine nature, man finds that the aura will quite naturally resemble the Presence in its radiant perfection. This is the pattern that appears in the heavens of God's consciousness and that can appear in the heaven of every man's consciousness; for it flows out from the seed pattern of perfection within man even as it manifests in the Presence above.

When Jesus said, "I and my Father are one,"[4] he referred to the balancing of the divine radiance of the God Presence and Causal Body within the outer manifestation, which through his reunion with reality had become one with God. Hence the color rays which had been focused through the "coat of many colors"[5] now became the nimbus, halo, or radiance of the Christ consciousness around him—the seamless garment that he wore as the Son of God.[6]

We have tried to make apparent in this discourse the fact that ordinary human beings are not endowed with this sense perception of the human aura, and this should always be borne in mind. Pilate heeded the dream of his wife, who warned him to have nothing to do "with that just man,"[7] more than the testimony of virtue manifest in the one who stood before him. He could find no fault with Christ Jesus;[8] but he did not bear witness to his perfection, else he would never have permitted the crucifixion of Christ, nor would he have turned him over to the Sanhedrin.

The commonsense approach to the realities of God is to be found in depth in the being of man. Man is a veritable treasure-house of beauty and perfection when he returns to the divine image — and I know of no better way to produce the miracle of the star of divine radiance in the human aura than to become one with God. This seemingly impossible hurdle is the panacea man seeks, and he shall find it if he seeks diligently enough and does not fear to surrender his little self; for all human ills will be cured by virtue of his becoming the Divine in manifestation. More harm has been done in the world by fraudulent readings of the human aura and false predictions based upon these readings than man is aware of. What a marvelous thing it will be when man turns his faculties of perception to the beholding of the reality of God in his very thought and standard!

Now I must, in defense of some arhats and advanced adepts upon the planet, affirm the accuracy of those who are able instantly to detect in depth the vibratory patterns manifesting in the world of others. It is incorrect to suppose that these will always speak out concerning their discernments. Naturally, gentleness and the will to see perfection supplant darkness will guide their motives and acts; but I solemnly warn here that whenever you are in the presence of a true adept or even an unascended being who has mastered many elements of perfection in his life, you should understand that if there is darkness of motive within you, he may see it or he may choose to ignore it.

By the same token, I solemnly warn those who fancy themselves adepts but who in reality have not overcome more than an iota of their imperfections and who have achieved in the eyes of God but a small portion of that which they imagine, to take heed that

they do not incorrectly discern, in their so-called readings of the lives of others, some quality that may not
even exist; for thereby some have brought great karma
down upon their heads.

All should exercise humility and care in placing
their value upon the development in the soul of the
higher consciousness of the God Presence, for this is
"without money and without price."[9] It is the invin-
cible attainment by which men become truly one with
God.

Devotedly, I AM

Kuthumi

V

The Intensification of the Aura

To the Devotee Who Would Make Contact with Our Brotherhood:

Man thinks of himself as solid. He lives within an envelope of flesh and blood that is penetrated by his consciousness. Consciousness must be regarded as man's connection with his Source, and its flexibility as man's greatest asset; yet when wrongly used, it is his greatest weakness. The consciousness of humanity today is so easily influenced by banal and barbaric doings that the magnificent cosmic purpose heaven has prepared in the creation of man is seldom recognized even minutely.

Man so easily becomes involved in the trivial manifestations of the footstool kingdom; and his in- doctrinations, being what they are, make him believe that the divine purposes and the doings of the ascended masters would not be to his liking. The singing of devotional songs, the chanting of holy man- tras, the engaging of the mind in spiritual conversa- tion and prayer to the Almighty are regarded today by the sophisticates as a milksop endeavor which could not possibly produce any good for them, but is reserved only for the weak-minded.

May I challenge this concept *in toto* and say that the greatest strength, the noblest ideal and truest valor, is to be found in the aspirant who ultimately achieves first his adeptship in his fulfillment of the divine plan, and then his eventual mastership in the ascension. Men erroneously think that only Jesus and a few other notable figures from the biblical centrum have ascended. How they would change their minds if they could see the cloud of witnesses above them in the heavens![1]

It is time that men understood the effects of their consciousness and their thoughts upon the human aura. I would go so far as to say that even their opinions have a strong influence upon them for good or for ill. I suspect that many have decided that I do not intend to discuss the negative aspects of the human aura. Perhaps they are right—we shall see. I am interested in stressing how that grandiose aura of the Christed one, surging with light, radiates out a divine quality in its very emanation that carries healing, nobility, honor, and cosmic strength to all who come in contact therewith. This aura of which I speak is not and never can be the product either of man's environment or of his social involvements. It is produced by divine doings, by entering into the cosmic consciousness of God through involvement with universal purpose, and especially by contact with our Brotherhood.

There is still too much vanity, however, in the whole business of God-seeking. There are times when we would gladly chasten men because of our great love for them, if doing so would stimulate a greater involvement in the only and true purpose behind the manifestation of their lives. Remember, the light shines in the darkness; and whereas the darkness comprehends it not,[2] those who do begin to open their understanding because this is their desire will find an absolute intensification of the light taking place within themselves. Hence a great deal more spirituality is involved in the God flame within the heart of each individual than he at first realizes.

In this very flame man has a catalyst posited right within himself, a sparkplug that can motivate him to make such attunement with his Presence whereby the magnificent influences of our Brotherhood can shine through his aura and he can become the outpost of heaven upon earth. Whoever said, and who dares to say, that any one person has the exclusive possession of this quality when it is the divine plan for all to radiate the one light? Just as man and all things were made by one Spirit, so the one Spirit expects all to enter in at the door. The door of the Christ consciousness literally trembles with anticipation of the moment when the individual will joyously enter into the sheepfold of his own reality.[3]

Probably some of you may wonder just what I am driving at and why, when I have offered to you studies on the human aura, I seem to be going around Robin Hood's barn. I can understand that, and I feel that now is the time for me to tell you that by this method I am seeking to develop a special quality in all of our students. That quality, which is of the Christ, will enable you to develop the kind of an aura that I will call *self-proving,* because it can be consciously intensified to do the most good.

In effect, man's aura is literally a broadcasting station for God's energy and his cosmic rays. Energies of light and the very thoughts of God himself and of the ascended masters combine with the benign thoughts that emerge from the very life plan of the individual and are then beamed or broadcast in all directions into the world of form. Those who are sensitive and can attune with these waves may perceive their nature and their origin, while those who do not understand cosmic law may become beneficiaries of these wondrous energies without ever knowing their source.[4] It makes little difference. We are concerned with overcoming the preponderance of human darkness that is abroad in the world today by literally flooding forth more light through the auras of many souls who shall dedicate their lives as outposts of cosmic regeneration to the planet.

Christ said, "I AM the light of the world: he that followeth me shall not walk in darkness."[5] When we speak of the light of the world, we speak of the light of the aura, and we are talking about a tangible manifestation. It is difficult for me to restrain myself when I hear the thoughts of individuals who carelessly read my words and then say, "What a nebulous concept he brings forth!" Contrary to their opinions, my concepts are incisive and they are given with a very definite purpose in mind and directly in accord with the one law of God. I say this because I am talking about permanent manifestations of universal grace; and withal I am trying to impress upon your minds the great fact that the law of God—the law of his love—is very much involved with the human aura. What is the human aura if it is not an extension into the world of form, into the universal web of the sum total of what the individual really is?

Well, then, if a man manifests a whimsical attitude, working his own or another's will without discrimination—sometimes good, sometimes bad or indifferent—can this be compared with the one who is literally harnessed to the divine dynamo and whose aura can be seen by those who truly see, as beginning to vibrate with the universal purpose? Not only do I know that these states of consciousness cannot be compared, but I know that one day in the changing consciousness of humanity the former will cease to be altogether. For God will win; of this I am certain. And those who follow the way of darkness because of the consuming of the thread of their own identity will ultimately be extinguished altogether by the very fires of creation;[6] for God is the Creator, the Preserver, and the Destroyer, and we have seen him in these and many guises.

In heaven's name, from whence cometh energy? What is it that beats your heart? A wish obviously not your own, or it would not so suddenly terminate. Instead, the will of God, the desire of God, beats your heart. Men's lives would not be paltry, then, if they also let him determine their consciousness and their thoughts.

Now that we have created a certain measure of understanding in many of our students about the factors that influence the human aura, we shall begin to show in greater detail the processes involved in broadcasting the qualities of the Christ so that great good can flow from your being out into the world in these troubled times and create in the brilliance of the sunshine a new awareness that fulfills the destiny of the children of men under the cosmic teachers for this age.

Extending my love to each of you, I hold the chalice of holy wisdom to be of special value in creating a new future out of which shall be born a greater summoning of understanding and its use. For knowledge must be correctly used and appropriated by transcendent magnificence rather than consumed on a few short years of sense pleasures without purpose.

The Brotherhood beckons to the many. The many can respond. If only the few do, I am certain we shall take delight in opening the curtain for them upon a new era of possibility. Let the weaving of regeneration begin anew the spinning of the tapestry of heaven's deepening involvement in the raising of humanity into

the folds of the Brotherhood, into the delight of
revealed purpose.

Firmly established in that purpose,
I remain

Kuthumi

VI

The Strengthening of the Aura

To the Student Willing to Experiment with Cosmic Law:

The thrust for a purpose envisioned by Master El Morya should be brought to bear not only upon the activities of the Brotherhood mutually coordinated on earth and in heaven, but also upon the life of each and every student. One of the first exercises I wish therefore to give to the students for the strengthening of the aura involves a threefold action. The student begins by visualizing the threefold flame expanding from within his heart;[1] he then seals himself and his consciousness in a globe of white fire; and when he is set, he proceeds to recite the following words with utter humility and devotion:

> I AM light, glowing light,
> Radiating light, intensified light.
> God consumes my darkness,
> Transmuting it into light.
>
> This day I AM a focus of the central sun.
> Flowing through me is a crystal river,
> A living fountain of light

That can never be qualified
By human thought and feeling.
I AM an outpost of the Divine.
Such darkness as has used me is swallowed up
By the mighty river of light which I AM!

I AM, I AM, I AM light.
I live, I live, I live in light.
I AM light's fullest dimension;
I AM light's purest intention.
I AM light, light, light
Flooding the world everywhere I move,
Blessing, strengthening, and conveying
The purpose of the kingdom of heaven!

As you visualize the cosmic white-fire radiance
around yourself, do not be concerned with the errors
in your thought that through the years may have in-
truded themselves upon your consciousness. Do not
allow yourself to concentrate upon any negative quality or condition. Do not let your attention rest upon
your supposed imperfections. Instead, see what the
light can do for you. See how even your physical form
can change, how a strengthening of the bonds of your
health can occur in body, mind, and spirit. Try this
exercise, simple though it may seem, and know that
many ascended beings will be performing it with you.

So many times adults fear to be thought childlike.[2] They would rather appear to be worldly-wise
and sophisticated—if they only knew that they are
running from deep-seated fears and insecurities which
they have buried beneath the clamor of social doings.
Surely with all they know about the physical universe,
their environment, and the patterns of the mind, they
must be able to reveal how great they really are! But,
dear hearts, what a shock some men and women are in
for when they shall come face to face with the blazing
truth of reality and realize that so much of what they

have learned must be unlearned and that what they
have thought to be their own greatness must be
sacrificed upon the altar of the true greatness of the
Christ Self. Then, perhaps, they will compare that
which they do not yet know with that which they do
know, and they will see how very lacking in luster they
are in the eyes of the cosmic hierarchy.

It is not needful to impress the masters with any
quality you may have. Heaven already knows exactly
what you are above and below. Heaven already knows
that you were made in God's image and likeness. If you
return to that image in a simple, sweet, and childlike
manner, I can promise you that heaven will not allow
you an overabundance of time in which to function in
the domain of the child, but it will elevate you into the
consciousness of a mature son or daughter of God.
While you maintain the attitude of the child, you will
be able to do something for yourself that will be both
valuable and valid; you will be able to loose the ties
that bind you to your egocentricities, until at last the
little bird of the soul shall flit into the heavens and
behold the glory of the eternal sun.

We in our Brotherhood of the Golden Robe are
devoted to the freeing of those who are yet enmeshed in
the vain aspects of the human consciousness. That they
may develop spiritually, free at last to express the
purposes of life as God intends them to do, is our
prayer. Many think it would be "so nice" if God would
speak the word and, suddenly, as with the rushing of a
mighty wind, all could speak the heavenly language.[3]
Men forget the karmic patterns that others have
carelessly woven and even the patterns that they
themselves have woven. They forget that these are the
self-made prison walls that keep them from discovering
the delights of heaven and from becoming gods among
men. They do not understand that this planet is a
schoolroom and that in these latter days many have

permitted their consciousness to grow dark even while knowledge seems increased across the land.

The knowledge that is important is the knowledge whereby man becomes first the master of his own consciousness and then the master of his world. Whereas in a relative sense one man may attain greater mastery than another in the manipulation of energy within a finite circle, this in no way guarantees that the big frog in the little pond will be able to navigate in the circle of the infinite. We are concerned with the measure of a man's advancement according to the divine precepts of the Brotherhood, which have been established under the guidance of the eternal Father from the beginning. We are interested not in generation, but in regeneration.

Now I am well aware that for some of our readers it is even a new idea that their thoughts can impinge upon others or that the thoughts of others can influence their own moods and manner of life. Nevertheless, it is so. The wise will therefore seek scientific methods of dealing with the problems of auric influences and thought penetration. If everyone knew how to use the tube of light and the violet consuming flame and believed in this method of self-transformation, I am certain that the world would be a different place.[4] The dissemination of such practical knowledge is invaluable when it is applied by those who receive it; hence I urge those disciples who have been calling for more light to be alert to properly use that which we shall release as they practice the aforementioned exercise.

So many misalignments in the human aura, so many nodules of dark and shadowed substance continually spew out their pollutants into the mainstream of man's energy, sapping his strength and weakening the entire manifestation of his life, that there is a great need for the flushing-out of darkness by a bubbling action of the light. Naturally, I am concerned that we first clear up these centers of shadow — the shadow of misqualification that is within man — before we energize the consciousness of our students. This problem sometimes presents a moot point; for those who pray often, who decree much, who love much, who involve themselves with the whole repertoire of the mantras of our Brotherhood seldom realize that as they gain in the power aspect of God, or even the love aspect of God, they also need the holy wisdom that shall direct their proper use of their forte of energy.

To misuse energy, to send out enormous power into the world like billowing storm clouds, is not the fulfillment of the divine intent. Energy should be directed as the perfect day coming from heaven into the lives of all it contacts. Let radiant blue skies and golden drops of sunlight pour through the foliage of man's consciousness, increasing the green, the beauty, and the color of the day of perfection in all men's thoughts.

May I chasten some by pointing out that sometimes knowingly and sometimes unknowingly you are using the energy of God to further your own moods and feelings in the world of form. Try God's way, the way of perfection;[5] for just as the Christ consciousness is the mediator between God and man,[6] so man can become a joint mediator with Christ; and inasmuch as he does what he wills with the energy God gives him, he controls, in a relative sense in the world of form, a portion of the divine energy for the entire planet. When he realizes this, the whole foundation of his life can be altered if he wills it so. This thought is injected as a direct quote from a conversation I had with beloved Morya, and I trust that the students will take it to heart.

What a wonderful opportunity lies before you as a gift from God as you correctly use his energy. Why, you can literally mold yourself and the whole world in the divine image! The potential for goodness lying within man is wondrous indeed; and as he learns how to properly extend and guard his auric emanations, he will realize more and more of that potential.

We shall do our part to make known the wondrous kingdom of heaven to as many as we possibly can. Will you help us to reach out in God's name, as his hands and feet, to lovingly become more and more the manifestations of the grace of God? The auric cloud glows; the auric cloud grows; the beauty of the kingdom of heaven solidifies in man as he gains a greater understanding of his own real nature.

Serenely in the light of purpose,
I remain

Kuthumi

VII

The Expansion of the Aura

To You Who Would Let Your Light Shine:
Coalescing around the spinal column are little portions of magnetic energy which I choose to call pieces of human destiny. As a man thinks, so is he.[1] As a man feels, so is he. As a man is, so goes his relationship with God, with purpose, and with the whole domain of life. The fabric of a man's being is composed of minutiae. The fabric of a man's being is composed of thought, and thought is indeed made up of the same substance as that faith once delivered unto the saints.[2]

Now as we recognize the need to let the sense of struggle cease, we want the students to develop in their consciousness the living tides of reality that flex the muscles of true spiritual being, enabling it to take dominion over the earth. Just as Christ walked upon the waters, so humanity must learn the way of the possessor of light. It has been said that the way of the transgressor is hard,[3] but those who possess the divine potential and exercise it in the divine way are in contact with the cloud of witnesses[4] that from spiritual realms extend the energies of the purpose of God to the earth.

There is a time in the lives of most children when heaven seems very near. Their journeys through the portals of life and death reveal the celestial truth of soul-knowing often forgotten with the passing of the years. Contact with heaven through the reestablishment of the threads of light between the heart and being of man and the living Father is beautiful and necessary if the world is to mature into an age of renewed innocence and tenderness expressed by mankind toward one another. Grace is a very special quality of God that charges the aura with a buoyant and joyous expression of heaven's beauty and wonder continuously expressed here below and continuously expressed above.

There is neither boredom nor unhappiness in the celestial state, but only a joyous sense of ongoingness that knows no defeat of sordid thought nor shame in its reflections. The miracle of eternity is caught in the web of time as man momentarily understands the power of his influence at the courts of heaven—as he realizes through oneness with his Christed being that he is the maker of his own destiny.

How much help is given and how much help can be evoked from the Universal is a subject in its own right. Yet I feel the need to assert on behalf of the students everywhere their friendship with those who dwell in the ascended master consciousness, in the Christ consciousness, a friendship maintained through the liaison of the angelic hosts and God-free beings and even the tiny elementals who are involved in the very outworkings of physical manifestation.

The words of the Psalmist "For he shall give his angels charge over thee. . .lest thou dash thy foot against a stone"[5] are intended for every son of God. Yet the temptation to command that these stones be made bread, for the purpose of assuaging mortal hunger, is very great; nevertheless, every son of God must be

prepared to overcome this temptation as the Master
did when he rebuked the lie of the carnal mind with
the words "It is written, Man shall not live by bread
alone, but by every word that proceedeth out of the
mouth of God."[6] Just as the world has its conspiracies
practiced against the sons and daughters of God by
those conspirators of Satan whose lives are literally
snuffed out without their ever knowing the end from
the beginning, so heaven has its own conspiracy of
light; and its emissaries are conspiring to evolve the
wondrous God-designs which the Father hath prepared
for them that love him.[7]

Now as the celestial bower is momentarily lowered
into view, the shape of things to come is revealed

When God does do his perfect work as planned
To right the wrongs of men by soul demand
And newly bring to view the hopes the ages sought
But never understood —
   the love and sacrifice he bought
To gather sheep and consecrate all lives
To higher goals and drives
   they little understood.
He vowed the plan to sweep from man
That hoary dust of ages overlaid,
To make men unafraid.
By love he showed to them
   that they should understand
The power of the pen
   that's mightier than the sword
And teaches all that I AM casting out all fear
From those who call upon me, far and near.
My light beams like a star of hope,
Dimension's newest opening
   upon the words I spoke;
For there is hope for all
Beneath the sun and star, or even moon.

For all things neath thy feet
Reveal the way complete
Is ever found within my Word,
The precious bread I broke;
For thou art mine and I AM thine—
Our living souls awoke.
Oh, see the magnet purpose,
　　glorious connecting chain,
Eternal joy revealed as love does ever reign!

Devoted ones, the pathway to the stars is found in
the thread of light anchored within the heart whence
the individual auric pattern expands naturally. Man
has so often been concerned with the concepts and
the many manifestations of the human aura—how
to protect it, how to direct it, how to increase it, how
to see it, how to interpret it—that he has seldom
taken into account these simple words Jesus long
ago revealed, "Let your light so shine before men. . . ."
This light of which he spake is the light which can be
magnetized through the human aura; for it is the
human emanation which heaven would make divine.
Therefore, "let your light so shine before men, that
they may see your good works and glorify your Father
which is in heaven."[8]

In our *Studies of the Human Aura,* which are
given to those who journey to our retreats as well as to
you who are fortunate to receive our weekly instruction, we seek to promote the same understanding that
Jesus imparted to his disciples—sometimes through
parable, sometimes through objective analysis of themselves and their contemporaries, sometimes through
direct teachings on the law which he read to them
from the archives of the Brotherhood. His entire effort
was to demonstrate what man can do and what man
can be when he unites with the God flame. And I say
to you today that it is to be, it is *be-ness,* it is to under-

stand that you are a ray of intense light that cometh
from the central sun into the world of form. This is
the key to creative mastery.

You must understand that you can draw forth
renewed magnificence and devotion to the cause of
your own immaculate freedom, and that this freedom
can be a crystal river flowing out from the throne of
God through your aura — which you have consecrated
as a vessel of the Holy Spirit — and into the world of
men. You must understand that wherever you go, your
opportunity to let your light shine — your aura — goes
with you, and that because you *are,* because you have
being and are being, you can take the sling of enlightened fortune and fling into the world, with almost
delirious abandon, your cup of joy that runneth over
in simply being a manifestation of God. You must
increase your understanding of the magnificence of
flow — the flow of the little electrons in their pure, fiery
state that seem to dance with total abandon and then
again to march like little soldiers in precision for-
mation — now disbanding as they assume what at first
may seem to be erratic shapes, now regrouping in their
intricate geometric patterns.

Purposefully man pours out into the universe the
healing balm that is his Real Self in action. Its flow is
guided by the very soul of the living God, by an innate
and beautiful concept of perfection steadily emanating
to him and through him. Does man do this? Can man
do it of himself? Jesus said, "I can of mine own self do
nothing; but the Father that dwelleth in me, he doeth
the works."[9] Understand that the inner fires banked
within yourself by the fire of the Holy Spirit can be
expanded by your own desire to be God's will in action.
Understand that these fires will act as a divine magnet
to increase the flow of perfection into your aura and
thence into the world. Understand that you must
therefore wax enthusiastic about daily expanding your

light through your meditations upon the Holy Spirit.

Because it is our belief that men would do better if they knew better, we have written this series even as we long ago dedicated our service to the enlightenment of the race. It is our desire to teach men that the human aura need never be a muddied sea, but can ever be an eternal *seeing* into the streams of immortal perfection whence cometh each man's being. One of the facts men should understand is that along with the pollution of their consciousness with impure thoughts and feelings and the emanations of the mass mind, which seem to take possession of the very fires of being and entrap them within imperfect matrices, is their desire for self-perpetuation. Hence, often the little, pitiful, dark-shadowed creatures of human thought and feeling will clothe themselves with a sticky overlay of qualities and conditions calculated to preserve the loves of the little self—thereby gaining acceptance in the consciousness bent on its own preservation. This is done in order to obscure the light of truth and to impugn it by reason of its very simplicity and perfection.

Do not be deceived. The light is yours to behold. The light is yours to be. Claim it. Identify with it. And regardless of whether or not men may mock simplicity, be determined in your childlike efforts to mature in God. One day the Divine Manchild will come to you, and the aura of the living Christ will be yours to behold and to be. To follow him in the regeneration is to follow him in the sun tides of the light that he was, that he is, that he ever shall be. You cannot cast yourself upon the rock and not be broken. But this is preferable to having the rock fall upon you and grind you to powder.[10]

There are more things in heaven than men on earth have dreamed of;[11] yet wondrous threads and penetrations have occurred and many have come home. We await the redemption of the world and we need in our Brotherhood those who, while having fallen in error, can simply trust and place their hand in ours as in the hand of God. For then the shuttle of the highest cosmic workers can move to and fro, from above to below, to carry greater instruction to the race of men, to the fountain of the individual life, where the shield of the aura is esteemed for the wonder God has made it.

Next week let us talk about the shield of the aura. God be with you each one.

I remain

Kuthumi

VIII

The Shield of the Aura

To Those Who Are Learning the Control of Energy:
     Some men upon the planet are little aware of the
need for protection to the consciousness; nor are they
aware of the possibility of others creating a barrage of
negative energy calculated to disturb the equilibrium
of their lifestreams. Let us set the record straight.
There are many who are at various stages of mastering
the control of negative energy and manipulating their
fellowmen by a wide range of tactics and techniques.
There are also spiritual devotees of varying degrees of
advancement who are in the process of mastering the
godly control of energy and who understand somewhat
the Brotherhood's systems of protection and the coun-
termeasures they can take in defense of their own life
plan.
     A God-endeavor indeed! Upon this earth, heaven
needs many who can work the handiwork of God. If a
planet is to fulfill its destiny, it must have those who
can work in the light of God that never fails,
unhampered by the forces of antichrist that would, if
they could, tear down every noble endeavor of the sons
and daughters of God. From time to time these are and

will be viciously assaulted through psychic means whereby the garments of their individual auras are sometimes penetrated and even rent, unless they are spiritually fortified. Yet that blessed aura, when it is properly intensified and solidified with light, becomes the shield of God against the intrusion of all negative energy, automatically and wondrously repelling those arrows that fly from the dark domain,[1] seeking to penetrate the peace of God that abides within, hence destroying peace.

Let me remind all of the natural envelope of invulnerability that serves as the protection of every man against those arrows of outrageous fortune[2] that fly so loosely in the very atmosphere of the planet betwixt men. However, through extraordinary measures the forces of darkness are often able to engage men in some form of argument whereby through inharmony they momentarily forfeit their protection. This is the game they play to catch men with their guard down; then again, they launch such an attack of viciousness as to cause them, through fear, to open up their worlds to discordant energies, which results in the rending of their garments.

Earlier in the series I gave an exercise for the strengthening of the aura through the development of the consciousness of invulnerability. Now I would make plain that in addition to spiritual fortitude one must also have spiritual reserves — what could almost be called reserve batteries of cosmic energy. The storing-up of God's light within the aura through communion with the Lord of hosts and through invocation and prayer, plus the sustaining of the consciousness in close contact with the angels, with the tiny builders of form acting under divine direction, and with all who are friends of light, creates an alliance with the forces of heaven. Through contact with each devotee's aura, these veritable powers of

light can then precipitate the necessary spiritual
fortifications that will give him a more than ordinary
protection in moments of need.

Let the student understand that his protection is
threefold: First of all, he enjoys, by the grace of God,
the natural immunity of the soul, which he must not
forfeit through anger or psychic entrapment; then
there is the assistance of the angelic hosts and cosmic
beings with whom he has allied himself and his forcefield through invocation and prayer; and last, but
certainly not least, there is the opportunity to request
of his own Presence the continuation of godly defense
through an intensification of the tube of light that will
also establish in his aura the needed protective strata of
energy which create a protective concept that cannot
be penetrated.

Bear in mind that sometimes the best defense of
man's being is a necessary offense. And when you find
that it becomes necessary to momentarily engage your
energies in this way, try to think of what the Master
would do, and do not allow your feelings to become
negative or troubled by your contact with human
discord of any kind. If you will consciously clothe
yourself with the impenetrable radiance of the Christ,
asking yourself what the Master would do under these
circumstances, you will know when to take the stand
"Get thee behind me, Satan!"[3] and when to employ the
tactic of gently holding your peace before the Pilate of
some man's judgment.[4]

Remember always the goal-fitting that is required
of those who would remain on the path. You did not
begin upon the path in order to become involved in
strife. You began in order to find your way back home
and to once again hold those beautiful thoughts of
celestial fortitude and cosmic intelligence that would
create in you the spirit of the abundant life. Birthless,
deathless, timeless, eternal, there springs from within

yourself the crystal fountain of light ever flowing, cascading in its own knowingness of the joys of God that create a chalice from which can be drunk the very water of life.[5] Freely you have received and freely you must give,[6] for the heart of each man can gather quantities without measure of this infinite love in its superabundant onrushing.

There is an erroneous thought in man that I must decry. It is the idea that man can get too much of spirituality. Oh, how fragile is the real thought of truth about this subject, and how easily it is shattered by human density and the misappropriation of energy. Man can never secure too much of God if he will only keep pace with him — with his light, with his consciousness, with his love. It is up to each one to do so, for no one can run the eternal race[7] for you. You must pass through the portals alone; you must be strengthened by your own effort. And you must also face the dragons of defeat and darkness that you once allowed free rein in your own arena of thought and feeling. Slay these you must by the sword of spiritual discrimination, thus building an aura of use to the Masters of the Great White Brotherhood.

Of what use is an electrode? Like the hard tip of a penetrating arrow flying through the air, an electrode becomes a point of release of giant energies that leap forth to conquer. And there are many things that need to be conquered. Above all, there are within oneself conditions of thought and sensitivities of feeling that require man's dominion. The man of whom I speak is the heavenly man — the man who abideth forever, one with God as a majority of good. His heart must not be troubled. And the injunction of the Master "Let not your heart be troubled"[8] must be heeded. For the aura is a beautiful electrode that can become of great use to heaven, and it must be consciously strengthened if man is to truly realize his potential.

Won't you understand with me the need to be the shield of God, to remain unmoved regardless of what conditions or difficulties you may face? For it is the power of heaven that liveth in you to strengthen the emanation of light from your being, both from the within to the without and from the without to the within. You can receive, both from without and from within, of the strengthening light that maketh man truly aware that he can be, in his aura and in his very being of beings, a shield of God—impenetrable, indomitable, and victorious.

I remain firm in the love of the purpose of your being,

Kuthumi

IX

The Protection of the Aura

To Men Who Would Entertain Angels:

Beware of those who by intellectual argument or religious dogma seek to destroy your beautiful faith in the gossamer-veiled protection of the angels! By his unbelief, man has failed to realize the magnificent protection that the human aura can receive from the angelic hosts. By his lack of recognition and his lack of attunement, he has allowed himself to pass through many harrowing experiences which could have been avoided by a simple cry for assistance to these beings whom God ordained from the foundation of the world to be his swift messengers of love, wisdom, and power.

Have you thought upon the love, wisdom, and power that the angels convey? May I suggest that you do it today. For over the track of your thoughts and the extension thereof into spiritual realms, over the swift and well-traveled pathways of the air, these infinite creatures of God's heart, serving so gloriously in his name and power, fly on pinions of light to do his bidding and to respond to your call. What a pity it is that some men lack the sweet simplicity of heart and mind that would allow them to speak unto the angels!

By their sophistication, their worldly-wise spirit, their hardness of heart, and their refusal to be trapped by the "plots" of heaven, they literally cut themselves off from so much joy and beauty; and their lives are barren because of it.

Will you, then, begin today the process of initiating or intensifying your contact with the angelic hosts as a means of fortifying your aura with what amounts to the very substance of the outer corona of the flame of God's own reality directed and glowing within the auric fires of the angelic hosts? How they love to receive the invitation of mortal men who desire to align themselves with the purposes of God! And do you know, these powerful beings cannot fail in their mission when they are invited by an embodied flame of light, a son of God, to come and render assistance!

Once mankind understand this fact—that the angelic hosts will respond to their calls—once they understand that these emissaries of heaven are bound by cosmic law to respond to their pleas and to send assistance where it is needed, they will also realize that even Christ availed himself of the ministrations of the angels throughout his life. Standing before Pontius Pilate, he said, "Thinkest thou that I cannot now pray to my Father, and he shall presently give me more than twelve legions of angels?"[1] The angelic hosts are the armies of God, the power, the service, the perfection, and the strength of God, flowing from the realm of immortality into immediate manifestation in the mortal domain, establishing the needed contact between God and man.

Consider for a moment how the Master employed the angelic hosts, not only in Gethsemane but also in his healing ministry, how he remained in constant attunement with them, acknowledging their presence in a spirit of oneness and brotherhood, esteeming them as the messengers of his Father. By startling contrast, the spurning of the angelic hosts by an ignorant humanity has caused many to fall under the negative influences of the dark powers that hover in the atmosphere, seeking to destroy mankind's peace, power, and purity.

I cannot allow this series to terminate without sounding the trumpet of cosmic joy on behalf of the angelic hosts. Many of us who are now classified as saints by some of the Christian churches[2] invoked the angels when we, as spiritual devotees, offered ourselves unto Christ in the service of humanity, knowing full well that of ourselves we could do nothing. Therefore, we looked to the assistance of the angelic hosts as God's appointed messengers. We did not expect God himself to come down into the everyday situations we encountered that required some special ministration from heaven; but we knew that he would send legions in his name, with the seal of his authority and power, to do his bidding.

How tragic it is that some men, through the puffiness of human pride, will speak only to God directly, thereby ignoring those whom God has sent, including the ascended masters and the sons and daughters of God upon the planet to whom is given a special ordination of conveying the message of truth unto humanity. It is so unnecessary for a distraught humanity engaged in numerous wars and commotions betwixt themselves to also launch an offensive against those who in truth defend every man's Christhood in the name of God.

To go forth with his power and in his name is a calling of considerable magnitude. May our protection abide with the Brothers of the Golden Robe serving at unascended levels, who in wisdom's gentle name would teach men the truth of the ages and thereby receive within their auras that celestial song that is the glory of God in the highest and the peace of God on earth to all

men of good will.[3] The message of the angels that rang
out over the plains of Bethlehem at the birth of Christ
has since been heard by the few in every century who
have communed with the angel ministrants; yet the
light of the angels is for all.

How could it be that we would so carelessly forget,
as mankind have done, the service and the devotion
of the angels directed from an octave of power and
beauty interpenetrating your own? Will you, then,
consider in the coming days and throughout your
whole life the blessed angels — not only the mighty
archangels, but also the cherubim and seraphim? For
there are many who will reach up to the great archangels, such as the beloved Michael, Chamuel, and
Uriel, without ever realizing that even they in their
great God-estate have their helpers who, in the perfor-
mance of their novitiate and in their own aspirations to
rise in the hierarchy of angels, will do almost any
divine kindness on behalf of the children of God on
earth when called upon by them to do so. All should
understand, then, the need to make the request. For
heaven does not enter the world of men unbidden, and
the tiniest angel in all of heaven welcomes the love and
invitation of men to be of service.

The information I have given you this week can
help you to consummate in your life the building and
charging of an aura with a radiance so beautiful that
as it sweeps through your consciousness, it will sweep
out the ignorance of the human ego and replace it with
the light of the Christ. Wherever you move, God
moves; and his angels accompany him. Let your auras
be charged with such purity and determination to do
the will of God and to be an outpost of heaven, that if
your shadow should but fall upon another whom God
has made, healing, joy, beauty, purity, and an extension of divine awareness would come to him.

You belong to God. Your aura, the garment of

God given to you, was designed to intensify his love. Do not tear it; do not carelessly force it open; but as a swaddling garment of love and light, keep it tightly wrapped around you. For one day, like the ugly duckling that turned into a swan, the aura will become the wedding garment of the Lord—steely white light reinforced by the divine radiance that no man can touch—that literally transforms the outer man into the perfection of the Presence, preserved forever intact, expanding its light and glowing as it grows with the fires of home and divine love.

Graciously, I AM

Kuthumi

X

The Purification of the Aura

To the Neophyte Who Is Ready to Be Purged by the Sacred Fire:

Remember that your aura is your light. Remember that Christ said: "Ye are the light of the world. A city that is set on an hill cannot be hid. Neither do men light a candle and put it under a bushel, but on a candlestick; and it giveth light unto all that are in the house."[1] Remember that he left this timeless advice as a means of inculcating into the consciousness of the race the inner formula for the proper employment of the human aura.

How many men have misunderstood what the aura is and what it can do! The aura is the sum total of the emanation of individual life in its pure and impure state. Often gently concealing from public view the darker side of human nature, the aura puts forth its most beautiful pearly-white appearance before men as if mindful of the words of God that have come down from antiquity "Though your sins be as scarlet, they shall be as white as snow."[2]

Occasionally the aura will momentarily turn itself inside out, and the more ugly appearance of a man's nature will come to the fore and be seen by those who are sensitive enough to perceive the human aura. This shouting from the housetops[3] of a man's errors ought not always to be deplored; for when the gold is tried in the fire of purpose, the dross often comes to the surface to be skimmed off. Therefore, when from time to time some negative influence appears in yourself or in someone else, consider it not as a permanent blight, but as a thorn which you can break off and remove from the appearance world. The fact that the within has thrust itself to the surface is an application of the principle of redemption; and when properly understood, this purging can mean the strengthening of your aura and your life.

As a part of the blotting-out process in the stream of time and space, dear hearts, God, in his greater wisdom, often uses exposure to public view or to your own private view as a means of helping you to get rid of an undesirable situation. Have you ever thought of that? What a pity if you have not. Suppressing evil or driving it deep within, tucking it away as though you would thereby get rid of it, does not really do the trick; for all things ought to go to God for judgment — willingly, gladly, and freely.

Men ought not to remain burdened by the inward sense of guilt or nonfulfillment that the suppression of truth often brings. For the cleansing of the human aura of these undesirable conditions need not be a lengthy process. Just the humble, childlike acknowledgement that you have made an error and the sincere attempt to correct it will do much to purify your aura. God does not angrily impute to man that which he has already done unto himself through the misuse of free will; for man metes out his own punishment by denying himself access to the grace of God through his infringement of the law. Therefore, the gentle drops of mercy and of God's kindness to man are offered as the cleansing agent of his own self-condemnation. They are like a heavenly rain, refreshing and cool, that is not denied to any.

Fill your consciousness, then, with God-delight, and observe how the purification of the aura brings joy unto the angels. Have you never read the words of the Master "Joy shall be in heaven over one sinner that repenteth, more than over ninety and nine just persons, which need no repentance"?[4] Oh, what a wonderful world will manifest for humanity when the power of God literally rolls through the heart and being of man untrammeled, flooding the planet with light! Yes, a great deal of instruction will still be needed; for there are so many things that we would reveal, not even dreamed of by the masses; and there is so much ongoingness in the Spirit of the Lord that my enthusiasm knows no bounds.

Yet mankind should understand that until they have prepared themselves for the great wedding feast to which they have been bidden,[5] they cannot fully know the meaning of the ongoingness of life; for the dark dye of human sorrow and degradation creates such a pull upon the consciousness that it is difficult for man to recognize the bridegroom in his God Self. Alas, man, although heavenly by nature, has through the misuse of free will decreased the natural, God-given vibratory rate of his atoms to such a low point that even the body temple must be broken again and again in order to arrest the cycles of the sense of sin. This breaking of the clay vessel affords him the opportunity to catch glimpses of reality, which he would never do—unless he had first attained self-mastery—if his life were to continue indefinitely in one physical body.[6]

How deep and how lovely are the mercies of God! How carefully he has provided for the gift of free will to man so that through the making of right choices man can find his way to the throne of grace and there receive the affirmation of his own God-given dominion, "Thou art my Son; this day have I begotten thee."[7] I am also reminded of the many devoted souls who through the ages have suffered the condemnation of their fellowmen as the result of the misunderstanding of their devotion to purpose. Like Joan of Arc and others who revealed a fiery determination for heaven to manifest upon earth, these great spirits have received little welcome from their peers and little understanding of their mission.

Let us hope together for the world that through the spreading-abroad of the balm of Gilead and the mercy of God as an unguent of healing, mankind will become unflinching in their devotion to cosmic purpose, even as we intensify our love through the student body. Tearing down any altars you may have erected in the past to the false gods of human pride and ambition and surrendering your momentums of failure to apprehend your reason for being, you will turn now with your whole heart to the development of the most magnificent focus of light right within your own aura.

Oh, I know something about the angstrom units, about the vibratory rate of the aura, about its impingement upon the retina of the eye and the interpolation of auras. I know about the subtle shadings that indicate gradations of tone in the thoughts and feelings of the individual which vacillate as a spunky wind or a frisky colt that has never been ridden. But how much better it is when, rather than label these as typical of the life pattern of another, men see at last the original image of divine perfection which God himself has placed within the human aura. For in most people some light can be perceived as a point of beginning, as a vortex around which greater light can be magnetized.

How much better it truly is when men hold the

immaculate concept for one and all and concern themselves not with the probing of the aura, but with the amplification of all that is good and true about the real man. I do not say that advanced disciples should not use methods of discrimination to discern what is acting in the world of another at a given moment or that the soul does not use these methods to give warning and assistance to other lifestreams; nevertheless, those who are able to discern the face of God in the face of man can retain the perfect image and assist the cosmic plan even while correctly assessing the present development of a lifestream. To hold faith in the purposes of God for another until that one is able to hold it for himself is to ally one's energies with the omnipotence of truth, which intensifies both auras in the richness of cosmic grace even as it intensifies the aura of the whole planet.

I want to bring to every student the realization that just as there is the flame of God in the individual aura, so there is the flame of God in the aura of the planetary body. Every act of faith you perform adds to the conflagration of the sacred fire upon the planet, just as every act of desecration tears down the great cosmic fortifications so gently and carefully builded by angelic hands who join with men and masters in service to life. Let all understand the building of the cosmic temple within the microcosm and the Macrocosm. The cosmic temple of the aura is an enduring edifice of the sacred fire. The cosmic temple of the world is made up of many auras dedicated to the indwelling Spirit of the Lord. Illumined thoughts and illumined feelings will enable individual man and humanity, striving together as one body, to cast into the discard pile those thoughts and feelings and actions not worthy to become a part of the superstructure of the temple of being.

Oh, be selective! Oh, be perfective in all your

doings! For someone is assigned to watch and wait with you until the moment comes when you can watch and wait with others. Just as the buddy system is used between soldiers in battle and between law-enforcement officers keeping the peace in your great cities, so there are cosmic beings, guardian angels, and lovely nature spirits of God's heart who watch over thee to keep thy way in peace and security, unmoved by mortal doings. For immortality shall swallow up mortality as death is swallowed up in victory,[8] and light shall prevail upon the planet.

The strengthening of the aura is a step in the right direction. Let none hesitate a moment to take it.

Devotedly and firmly I remain wedded
to the precepts of the Brotherhood,

Kuthumi

XI

The Star of the Aura

To Each One Who Will Wear the Garment of God:
    The garment of God is the most transcendent
man can ever wear. It represents the highest echelon of
life, the development not only of the love nature of
God and of the wisdom of God, but also of the element
of power. This so many seek without willing first to
make the necessary preparation in the refinements of
love and holy wisdom in manifestation within the soul.
How easy it is for individuals to accept primitive as well
as intellectual ideas that rationalize the thrust of ego
upon ego, without ever analyzing the attitude and the
aura of the masses, who are saturated with the concept
of oneness as the blending of human personalities. The
oneness men should seek to understand and manifest is
that of the individuality of God reflected in man.
Oneness in Spirit is ever consecration in the Gloria in
Excelsis Deo—the Glory to God in the Highest.
    Through the linking-together of the great and
the trivial in human consciousness, mankind defeat
evermore the manifestation of true spiritual transcen-
dence. The ongoingness of the nature of God as it
manifests in man is a study in individual development.

As one star differs from another star in glory,[1] so by the process of linking together the mediocrity of man and the sublimity of God, the latter is compromised beyond recognition. But only in the human consciousness does the ridiculous detract from the sublime. By the splitting of divine images and by the subtle process of image distortion resulting in the redistribution of the soul's energies according to astral patterns which nullify the original spiritual design, man begins to feel that the magnificence of cosmic ideas is in reality too far from him and the gulf between the human and the Divine too great; thus his consciousness remains in the doldrums of mortal experience.

Wise is the chela who guards against this invasion of the mind and heart, who recognizes those negative subtleties which seek to stealthily enter the aura and turn it from its natural brightness to darkening shadows of gray and somber hue. The strengthening of the bonds of the aura with light and virtue will enable the soul to leap as a young deer across huge chasms of erroneous ideas separating man from God when once the esteem of the immaculate concept is given preeminence in his consciousness. To involve oneself in the distractions of the world and to love the things of the world,[2] being consumed by them, deprive one of the magnificent occupation of seeking to become one with God, a cosmic occupation of permanent reality.

There may be a time to plant, to water, to love, and to die;[3] but we are concerned with the abundant life, which is nowhere more abundant than it is in the magnetic shower of Cosmic Christ power that pours forth to the individual from the heart of his own God-identity when he fixes his attention upon the Presence and understands that herein is his real, eternal, immortal, and permanent life. As long as he, like a potted plant, sits in the limited circle of his own individuality, he remains tethered to its ranges; but once he allows the power and the pressure of the divine radiance to descend from the heart of his God Presence, he becomes at last the recipient of immortal life in all of its abundance and unlimited outreach.

The illusion of the self must remain an illusion until the self is surrendered; therefore, men ready and willing to be delivered from the bondage of a self-centered existence into the infinite capacities of the God Self must surrender unconditionally to the Divine Ego. Then there is not even a sense of loss, but only of gain, which the soul perceives as cosmic worth as he increases his ability to develop in the aura the consciousness of the absolute penetration of the Absolute. Physically, the very atoms of man become drenched with a shower of cosmic wave intensity — the drinking of the elixir of life, the magic potion by which a man is transformed. In a moment, in the twinkling of an eye, the trump of true being sounds.[4] This is God, and no other will do.

The carnal mind cannot remain in command of the affairs of such a one. A Christ is born, a nova upon the horizon, one willing to follow in the footsteps of cosmic regeneration. Thus the purity and power of the Presence strike a new note, and old things truly pass away as all things become new.[5] The domain of destiny is all around us. As man evolves, so cosmic beings evolve — wheels within wheels, leading to the great hub of life and to the reality of spiritual contact as the *antahkarana* is spun, perceived, and absorbed.

How beautiful is contact with hierarchy, with the hand of those brothers of light whose garments are robes of light, whose consciousness, reflecting the anticipation of spiritual progress, is joyously attuned to those God-delights which remove from the mind of man the sense of the comparable or the incomparable. The world of comparison diminishes; the world of God appears. The aura is drenched with it — no sacrifice too great, no morsel too small to be ignored, no grasp too significant not to find its own integral pattern of usefulness. And so the domain of the human aura is lost in a sea of light, in the greater aura of God; the windows of heaven open upon the world of the individual, and the showers of light energy resound as an angelic choir singing of the fire of worlds without end.

The anvil of the present is the seat of malleability; all things less than the perfection of the mind of God mold themselves according to progressive reality, plasticity, the domain of sweetness, the chalice of new hope to generations yet unborn. The historical stream, muddied no longer, appears as the crystal flowing river from which the waters of life may be drunk freely.[6] The monad makes its biggest splash as it emerges from the chrysalis of becoming to the truth of living being as God intended.

Sensing the human aura as a star, man gains his victory as he sees the universe flooded with stars of varying intensity. By comparison his own auric light glows more brightly, for the fires of competition fan the flame of aspiration. But all at once he staggers with the realization that he is in competition with no one, for the incomparable mystery of his own exquisite being is revealed at last.

Questioning and doubts as to the purpose of life no longer engage his mind, for all answers are born in the ritual of becoming. The fascination of truth envelops him, and he weans himself from the old and familiar concepts that have stifled the glow of perpetual hope within his soul. He is concerned now that others shall also share in this great energy source of reality flowing forth from on high. Naught can transpire with his consent that God does not will, for the will of God and the will of man are become one.

When each man consents to this victory, the struggle lessens and then is no more; for faith in the fatherhood of God reconciles men through Christ to the fountainhead of their eternal purpose. The glow of a new hope, infusing all, lends direction to the expansion of the auric light. The forcefield is magnified, and in the magnification thereof the star of the man who has become one with God shines on the planes of pure being as the angels rejoice.

A new life is born — one for whom the expectancy of life will continue forever; for in the endlessness of cycles, the aura, as a glowing white-fire ball, a summer radiance of the fruit of purpose, continues to magnify itself in all that it does. God is glorified in the auric stream.

Next week we shall conclude our dissertation on *Studies of the Human Aura.* The richest blessings of our Brotherhood be upon all.

Devotedly, I AM

Kuthumi

Meditation on Self

I am no blight of fantasy —
    Clear-seeing vision of the Holy Spirit, being;
Exalt my will, desireless desire,
    Fanning flame-inspired fire, glow!
I will be the wonder of thyself,
    To know as only budding rose presumes to be.
I see new hope in bright tomorrow here today;
    No sorrow lingers, I AM free!
O glorious Destiny, thy Star appears,
    The soul casts out all fears
And yearns to drink the nectar of new hope;
    All firmness wakes within the soul —
I AM becoming one with thee.

XII

The Crystal Flowing Stream of the Aura

To Men and Women Desiring to Preserve the Immortal Soul Within:

The aura is a crystal flowing stream that issues from the heart of God. No negation is here: only an indomitable fountain continually pouring forth a steadfast stream of magnificent, gloriously qualified substance—the substance of life itself.

As a little child presents his first freshly picked bouquet of flowers to his mother, so the innocence of the child-mind tunes in with this crystal flowing stream of God's consciousness infusing the natural aura of God in man with the life that beats his heart.

O children of the day, the night should not be given preeminence! Your energy should become qualified by the eternal flow of hope that, if you will it, can enlarge its own opening into the fountain of your mind and heart—into the fountain of God's own mind and heart. Your mind must become the mind of Christ; the desire of your heart must become the desire of the Holy Spirit, flowing assistance to those awaiting the loving hand of perfection in their lives.

May I tell you that when you come in contact with

the dark and sullen auras of those who have misqualified the bulk of their energy throughout their
lives, you ought to recognize that in reality these are
not happy individuals. They may laugh, they may
dance, they may sing and make merry, they may wail
and utter lamentations—they may run the gamut of
human emotion; but they shall not prevail, for the law
inexorably returns to each one exactly that which he
sends out.

The way of perfection is the natural way of the
aura. But, almost as a mania, individuals seldom fail
to misqualify the energies of their lives, bringing their
very nerves into a taut state. They become like a
tightened spring of energy wound in erratic layers, and
they refuse the stabilizing influences of the Christ mind
and the divine heart. Having no other energy, they are
compelled to use this which they have locked in the coil
of their mental and emotional incongruities. Thus
through psychic imbalance, the spring is sprung and
the impure substance of the aura pours forth in a
putrid stream. All of the delicate refinements of the
soul and the natural culture and grace of the Holy
Spirit are spilled upon the ground; and the kingdom of
heaven is denied the opportunity to function through
the individual auric pattern.

To say that they suffer is an understatement; for
through their own denial of the hope of Christ they are
punished *by* their sins, not *for* them. The light of God
that never fails continues to flow into their hearts, but
it remains unperceived and unused; for instead of
flowing into vessels of virtue—those pure forms and
noble ideas that retain the light of God in man—it
is automatically channeled into the old and crusty
matrices formed in earlier years through ego involvement and contact with the forces of antichrist
that permeate society.

These patterns sully the descending light as dark

clouds that filter the sunlight of being and preclude the spiritual advancement of the soul. Yet in moments of naked truth, men and women admit their inner need, and their hearts and minds cry out for the preservation of the immortal soul within them. They fear the response of heaven; and, failing to recognize the all-pervading love of the Spirit, they watch helplessly as the soul, little by little, loses hold upon the steadily outpouring energies of life; for each misqualification brands them with the fruit of retribution.

While for a time it seems that those who dwell in error escape the wrongs they have inflicted upon others, let me remind you that life will make her adjustments and none shall escape the responsibility for their actions. As he whose voice was of one crying in the wilderness said, "[his] fan is in his hand, and he will thoroughly purge his floor, and will gather the wheat into his garner; but the chaff he will burn with fire unquenchable."[1]

We are not concerned with matters of crime and punishment, but with the joy and courage that are born in the soul through the crucible of experience — the courage to be the manifestation of God, the courage to walk in the Master's footsteps, to feel the surge of his hope wherever you are, and to know that even though you walk in the valley of the shadow, you will not fear,[2] because his light is surging through you.

Beware the sin of complacency and of passing judgment upon the lives of others. Before allowing your thoughts and feelings to crystallize around a given concept, ask yourself this question: Is the evidence indeed conclusive, and do you possess absolute knowledge concerning the motive of the heart and karmic circumstances surrounding other lives? If so, are you able to weigh these factors better than heaven itself? Wisely did the Master speak when he said, "Judge not, that ye be not judged."[3]

Therefore, point by point, let the Holy Spirit remold the vessels of thought and feeling that hinder your flight; and let the fruit of the crystal flowing stream, the fountainhead of life, be perceived for the diadem that it is—a crowning radiance that bursts around your head. Then the emanation of the Spirit Most Holy shall take dominion over all outer circumstances and, like the branches of a willow, trail upon the ground of consciousness by the still waters of the soul.

> The Lord comes down to the meek and lowly;
> His peace none can deny.
> His light that glows most brightly
> Is a fire in the sky.
>
> The children hear him coming,
> His footsteps very near;
> They 'wait his every mandate,
> His word "Be of good cheer."[4]
>
> They feel a joy in knowing
> That deep within their hearts
> There is a glimmer showing,
> Enabling all to start
>
> Release from all earth's bondage,
> Each weight and every care—
> Open sesame to being,
> Helping all to know and share.
>
> The Lord is in his heaven,
> So childlike is his love.
> The Christ, the heavenly leaven,
> Raises each one like a dove.
>
> His face in radiant light waves
> Is pulsing ever new;
> Freedom from past error
> He brings now to the few.

But many are the sheep,
His voice each one may hear;
This is his very message,
Wiping 'way each tear.

Oh, see him in the burdened,
The hearts o'erturned with grief,
The lips that mutter murmurs,
The tongues that never cease.

For social clamors babble,
Their judgments utter bold—
A child of light untrammeled,
A soul made of pure gold.

Each moment like a rainbow,
The presence ever near
Caresses in the darkness,
Bids all, "Be of good cheer."

Oh, take then life's great banner,
I AM God Presence true,
And hold me for the battle,
A victor ever new.

For life's own goalposts show me
The way I ought to go.
My hand is thine forever,
Enfold me with thy glow.

May all be reminded each day as they utter the
words of Jesus "Our Father which art in heaven"[5] or
any prayer, any call to God, that the aura is the
Father's light and that his Son has said to all, "Let your
light so shine before men, that they may see your good
works and glorify your Father which is in heaven."[6]
May the sweet concepts of the living Christ, recalling a
lost youth and the era of holy innocence, remind you of
life's noble opportunities to be the grace and sweetness
that you expect others to be.

Then, regardless of what men do unto you, you will know that what you do unto them is a part of the age to be, of a mastery to become, of an adeptship now aborning. Through night and day, through time and space, through life and death, you shall remain undismayed as the outpost of delight that melts away the darkness now gathering o'er the land. Thus shall the world's tears be wiped away as the mantle of God covers the earth. Everywhere through the night, let the shafts of light right where you are pierce the gloom of the world by the "good cheer" of the Master.

We, the brothers of our retreat, together with each Master, each angel, and each adherent of the sacred fire of the living God from their place in cosmos, beam our love to you wherever you are. We shall never forsake those who do not forsake the light of their own God Presence.

Eternal devotion,

Kuthumi

Notes

To Those Who Seek Self-Knowledge

1. Mal. 3:1-3.
2. John 1:9.
3. Exod. 3:14.
4. John 1:5, 14.
5. Matt. 3:2.
6. Luke 22:42.
7. Matt. 24:30.
8. Rev. 11:3.
9. Rev. 11:4.
10. Dan. 7:9.
11. Matt. 4:1-11.
12. Luke 9:29.
13. Matt. 24:35.
14. A. T. Barker, comp., *The Mahatma Letters to A. P. Sinnett from the Mahatmas M. and K.H.* (London: Rider and Co., 1923), p. 215.

Chapter I

1. Matt. 5:8.
2. Matt. 18:12.
3. Matt. 10:26.
4. Matt. 13:12.
5. Akashic records: The recordings of all that has taken place in an individual's world are 'written' by recording angels upon a substance and dimension known as akasha and can be read by those whose spiritual faculties are developed.
6. Matt. 18:10.
7. Matt. 25:40.
8. Col. 2:9.
9. Antahkarana: The web of perfection within the thread of light connecting each one with the heart of God.
10. John 8:12.

Chapter II

1. Overlaid with his imperfect thoughts and feelings.
2. Gen. 3:22; Rev. 22:14.
3. Luke 16:8.
4. John 14:12.
5. The basic precepts of the ascended masters' teachings given in their retreats are published in the Keepers of the Flame Lessons in the masters' own words; they provide an excellent foundation

for those taking up beloved Kuthumi's *Studies of the Human Aura.*

Chapter III

1. Pss. 1:2; Josh. 1:8.
2. Col. 2:9.
3. Rom. 8:17.
4. Matt. 7:3.

Chapter IV

1. Isa. 30:20.
2. 1 Cor. 6:20.
3. Matt. 7:1.
4. John 10:30.
5. Gen. 37:3.
6. John 19:23.
7. Matt. 27:19.
8. Luke 23:4.
9. Isa. 55:1.

Chapter V

1. Heb. 12:1.
2. John 1:5.
3. John 10:1.
4. See *Romance of Two Worlds* by Marie Corelli, available from The Summit Lighthouse.
5. John 8:12.
6. Isa. 1:28.

Chapter VI

1. The blue plume to one's left, the yellow in the center, and the pink plume to the right.
2. Matt. 19:14.
3. Acts 2:1-4.

4. This teaching of the Brotherhood is explained in the Keepers of the Flame Lessons.
5. Pss. 18:32.
6. 1 Tim. 2:5.

Chapter VII

1. Prov. 23:7.
2. Jude 3.
3. Prov. 13:15.
4. Heb. 12:1.
5. Pss. 91:11-12.
6. Matt. 4:3-4.
7. 1 Cor. 2:9.
8. Matt. 5:16.
9. John 5:30; 14:10.
10. Matt. 21:44.
11. William Shakespeare, *Hamlet,* act 1, sc. 5, lines 165-66.

Chapter VIII

1. Pss. 91:5.
2. William Shakespeare, *Hamlet,* act 3, sc. 1, line 58.
3. Luke 4:8; Matt. 16:23.
4. Matt. 27:13-14.
5. Rev. 22:17.
6. Matt. 10:8.
7. Heb. 12:1.
8. John 14:1.

Chapter IX

1. Matt. 26:53.
2. Kuthumi was embodied as Francis of Assisi (1182-1226), founder of the Franciscan order.
3. Luke 2:14.

555

5555555555555452545555525555555555555455555

Chapter X

1. Matt. 5:14-15.
2. Isa. 1:18.
3. Luke 12:3.
4. Luke 15:7.
5. Matt. 22:1-14.
6. The Master is speaking of the death process, given to man as an act of mercy that he might have a reprieve from the vanity of this world and partake of the light and wisdom of higher realms between embodiments; moreover, the forfeiting at birth of the memory of previous lives enables the hope of heavenly spheres to replace the seemingly endless records of mortal involvement.
7. Pss. 2:7.
8. Isa. 25:8; 1 Cor. 15:54.

Chapter XI

1. 1 Cor. 15:41.
2. 1 John 2:15.
3. Eccles. 3:1-8.
4. 1 Cor. 15:52.
5. 2 Cor. 5:17.
6. Rev. 22:17.

Chapter XII

1. Luke 3:17.
2. Pss. 23:4.
3. Matt. 7:1.
4. John 16:33.
5. Matt. 6:9.
6. Matt. 5:16.

YOUR DIVINE SELF

Plate 1

Chart of Your Divine Self

There are three figures represented in the chart, which we will refer to as the upper figure, the middle figure, and the lower figure. The upper figure is the I AM Presence, the I AM THAT I AM, God individualized for every son and daughter of the flame. The Divine Monad consists of the I AM Presence surrounded by the spheres (rings of color, of light) which comprise the causal body. This is the body of First Cause that contains within it man's "treasure laid up in heaven"—perfect works, perfect thoughts and feelings, perfect words—energies that have ascended from the plane of action in time and space as the result of man's correct exercise of free will and his correct qualification of the stream of life that issues forth from the heart of the Presence and descends to the level of the Christ Self.

The middle figure in the chart is the mediator between God and man, called the Christ Self, the Real Self, or the Christ consciousness. It has also been referred to as the Higher Mental Body. The Christ Self overshadows the lower self, which consists of the soul evolving through the four planes of Matter in the four lower bodies corresponding to the planes of earth, air, fire, and water; that is, the etheric body, the mental body, the emotional body, the physical body.

The three figures of the chart correspond to the Trinity of Father (the upper figure), Son (the middle figure), and Holy Spirit (the lower figure), which the evolving soul is intended to become and for whom the body is the temple. The lower figure is the nonpermanent aspect of being which is made permanent through the ritual of the ascension. The ascension is the process whereby the lower figure, having balanced his karma and fulfilled his divine plan, merges first with the Christ consciousness and then with the living Presence of the I AM THAT I AM. Once the ascension has taken place, the soul, the corruptible aspect of being, becomes the incorruptible one, a permanent atom in the body of God. The Chart of Your Divine Self is therefore a diagram of yourself—past, present, and future.

The lower figure represents mankind evolving in the planes of Matter. This is how you should visualize yourself standing in the violet flame, which you invoke in the name of the I AM Presence and in the name of the Christ in order to purify your four lower bodies in preparation for the ritual of the alchemical marriage—your soul's reunion with the Spirit, the I AM Presence. The lower figure is surrounded by a tube of light, which is projected from the heart of the I AM Presence in answer to your call. It is a field of fiery protection sustained in Spirit and in Matter for the sealing of the identity of the overcomer. The threefold flame within the heart is the spark of life projected from the I AM Presence through the Christ Self and anchored in the etheric planes in the heart chakra for the purpose of the soul's evolution in Matter. Also called the Christ flame, the threefold flame is the spark of man's divinity, his potential for Godhood.

The crystal cord is the stream of light that descends from the heart of the I AM Presence through the Christ Self, thence to the four lower bodies to sustain the soul's vehicles of expression in time and space. It is over this cord that the energy of the Presence flows, entering the being of man at the top of the head and providing the energy for the pulsation of the threefold flame and the physical heartbeat. When a round of the soul's incarnation in Matter-form is complete, the I AM Presence withdraws the crystal cord, the threefold flame returns to the level of the Christ, and the energies of the four lower bodies return to their respective planes.

The dove of the Holy Spirit descending from the heart of the Father is shown just above the head of the Christ. When the individual man, as the lower figure, puts on and becomes the Christ consciousness as Jesus did, the descent of the Holy Spirit takes place and the words of the Father, the I AM Presence, are spoken, "This is my beloved Son in whom I AM well pleased" (Matt. 3:17).

A more detailed explanation of the Chart of Your Divine Self is given in the Keepers of the Flame Lessons and in *Climb the Highest Mountain* by Mark and Elizabeth Prophet, published by The Summit Lighthouse.

The Ascended Masters Jesus and Saint Germain

The Ascended Masters Jesus and Saint Germain, passing the torch of the Christ consciousness and the I AM THAT I AM for the Piscean and Aquarian dispensations, stand in the long history of the earth and her evolutions as the great deliverers of nations and peoples by the sacred fire of freedom and the salvation of the soul through the path of the ascension. This is the path of initiation that leads to the soul's reunion with the I AM Presence through the mediator, the Christ Self—the open door of the eternal Christos which no man can shut—personified in the Christ flame of the Piscean Master Jesus. It is the path of initiation by the baptism of the sacred fire of the Holy Ghost revealed through the God consciousness of the Aquarian Master Saint Germain as he delivers to the people of God the dispensation of the seventh age and the seventh ray—the violet flame and its invocation through Father, Son, and Holy Spirit.

Saint Germain is the seventh angel prophesied in Revelation 10:7 who comes to sponsor the finishing of the mystery of God "as he hath declared to his servants the prophets." Saint Germain brings to the lost sheep of the house of Israel the remembrance of the name of the Lord God—I AM THAT I AM. This ascended master, who was embodied as the prophet Samuel, calls the Twelve Tribes from the four corners of the earth and makes known to them their true identity as the light-bearers commissioned to serve with the Ancient of Days to set the captives free by the Christ Self, their own Real Self—the Word that was the true light which lighteth every man that cometh into the world.

Jesus and Saint Germain, together with all of the heavenly hosts, ascended masters, Elohim, and archangels—the Spirit of the Great White Brotherhood—have come forth in this moment of the turning of the cycles of Pisces and Aquarius to teach us how to call upon the name of the Lord in order that we may overcome the dragon, the personification of evil, the *e-veil*, or *energy veil*, referred to in the scriptures as the carnal mind, the Devil, the Evil One, the Adversary, Lucifer, Satan, etc.

This great overcoming of the darkness by the light was prophesied by Jesus Christ to his disciple John as he wrote in the Book of Revelation: and they overcame him "by the blood of the Lamb, and by the word of their testimony." The blood of the Lamb is the essence, or "Spirit," of Christ which is his teaching withheld from the people for thousands of years by 'false Christs' and 'false prophets', now brought forth once again by the ascended masters and their messengers. The "word of their testimony" is the science of the spoken Word whereby through prayer, meditation, dynamic decrees, and communion with the Lord, his sons and daughters become the instrument of his Word as the fiat of the Logos.

Thus the knowledge of the true teaching of Christ—now brought to our remembrance, as Jesus promised, by the Holy Spirit in the person of the ascended masters as they release their dictations to the messengers—combined with the decrees of the Lord God, the I AM THAT I AM, spoken through the ascended masters and their unascended disciples, are the means whereby the light-bearers overcome the world tyranny of the fallen ones in this and every century. This Great Overcoming following the "Great Tribulation" is decreed by Almighty God as is the coming of the ascended masters, their messengers, and their disciples. It is the teaching and the mission of the Ascended Masters Jesus and Saint Germain that we must make every decree of the Lord our own and then stand fast to behold the salvation of our God.

As the deliverer of both Jew and Christian from the leaven—false doctrine of the Pharisees, ancient and modern—Jesus and Saint Germain

The Ascended Master Jesus Christ

The "Anointed One," World Saviour, World Teacher, Hierarch and Avatar of the Piscean Age; Great Exemplar of the Second Person of the Trinity and Personification of the Only Begotten Son of God; the Open Door to the Christ Consciousness Individualized as the Light, the Christ Self, of Every Child of God, Serving on the Sixth Ray (purple and gold) of Ministration and Service; Wayshower of Sons and Daughters of the Word Incarnate; Initiator of Souls on the Thirty-Three Steps of the Path of the Ascension

Plate 2

The Ascended Master Saint Germain

Chohan (Lord) of the Seventh Ray, Hierarch of the Aquarian Age, God of Freedom to the Earth, Sponsor of the United States of America, Great Alchemist and Dramatist of the Soul's Evolution through the Planes of Time and Space into the Great Sphere of Cosmic Consciousness, Initiator of Souls in the Science and Ritual of Transmutation through the Violet Flame of the Holy Spirit

Plate 3

proclaim the Messiah already come in the threefold flame of each one's heart and in Jesus who as the Son of God came to teach us the way of the Christ, personified not in himself alone but in every son and daughter of God. Thus in truth, and in the true science of the religion he taught, all mankind can and shall declare with the blessed Sons of God "I AM the way, the truth, and the life" and understand that it is the I AM THAT I AM, the Lord our God, dwelling in our own temple who is, was, and forevermore shall be the way, the truth, and the life.

The likenesses of Jesus and Saint Germain were painted by Charles Sindelar, famous American artist and illustrator of the 1920s and '30s. Jesus Christ appeared to the artist on twenty-two consecutive mornings at 2:00 a.m., and the image of the Master would appear throughout the day over both canvas and etching plate, distracting him from his work until he took the advice of a friend to "paint what you have seen." After five days of continuous work, the portrait was completed. Charles Sindelar was not satisfied with his rendering of the mouth and therefore on the fifth night at 2:00 a.m., Jesus returned until the artist had perfected on canvas the likeness of his master who stood before him.

The messengers testify that the portrait of Jesus is the exact likeness of the master as he has appeared to them both in the retreats of the Brotherhood, in their homes, and on the platform during dictations. They have confirmed that the portrait of Jesus depicts him as he appeared at the Royal Teton Retreat "in consultation with Saint Germain and the tall master from Venus."

A number of years after the painting of Jesus was completed, Saint Germain appeared to Charles Sindelar in the presence of Guy Ballard, and the artist completed the portrait as the messenger served as the anchor point to sustain the forcefield and the Electronic Presence of Saint Germain. Again the messengers have stated that this likeness of Saint Germain is indeed that of the ascended master who is their sponsor and the sponsor of America and every nation on earth. He has been known to devotees of freedom on the planet Earth for over seventy thousand years, and his great love and sacrifice has enabled the evolutions of earth to have the use of the violet flame for the transmutation of all misqualified energies of the human consciousness which stand between the soul and its salvation, *Self-elevation,* through the Christ personified in Jesus, the Saviour, the fullness of the Word incarnate.

The Ascended Masters Jesus and Saint Germain have given their life and their likenesses in these paintings as a glad, free gift for the salvation of earth and her evolutions and "that the earth may be filled with the glory of God as the waters cover the sea." Neither the masters nor their portraits can be confined to any creed, religion, doctrine, or dogma, nor can their names be invoked for the sealing of anyone's private interpretation of the law or the scriptures.

These blessed ascended masters are the intimate friend, guide, teacher, counselor, and comforter on the way of life, walking hand in hand with the light-bearers in this age. All who will call upon them in the name of the I AM THAT I AM will be blessed with an immediate manifestation of their Electronic Presence—the fullness of their tangible light body focalized in time and space within the aura of their disciple. The devotee may visualize himself with his right hand in the hand of Jesus and his left in the hand of Saint Germain. Calling upon these great wayshowers of the Twelve Tribes of Israel, devotees of truth may know with the certainty of cosmic law, whereby the call compels the answer, that these ascended masters will never leave him as long as he remains obedient to the principles and practice of Truth, Life, and Love, to the Law of the One, and to the inner God Flame, the I AM THAT I AM.

Glossary

Words set in *italics* are defined elsewhere in the Glossary

Adept. A true adept is an initiate of the *Great White Brotherhood* of a high degree of attainment; one undergoing advanced initiations of the *sacred fire* on the path of the *ascension*.

Akashic records. All that transpires in *Matter* is recorded in akasha — "etheric" energy vibrating at a certain frequency so as to absorb, or record, all of the impressions of life. These records can be read by those whose soul faculties are developed.

Angel. An 'angle' of God's consciousness; an aspect of his Self-awareness; an individualization of the creative fires of the cosmos. The angelic hosts are an evolution of beings set apart from the evolutions of mankind by their flaming selfhood and by their purity of devotion to the Godhead and to the God-free beings they serve. Their function is to concentrate, intensify, and amplify the energies of God on behalf of the entire creation. They minister to the needs of mankind by intensifying feelings of hope, faith, and charity, honor and integrity, truth and freedom, mercy and justice, and every aspect of the crystal clarity of the mind of God.

Angels are electrons revolving around the Sun Presence that is God — electrons who have elected to expand his consciousness in every plane of being. They are rods and cones of concentrated energy that can be diverted into action by the Christed ones wherever and whenever there is a need. There are angels of healing, protection, love, comfort and compassion, angels attending the cycles of life and death, angels who wield the flaming sword of truth to cleave asunder the real from the unreal. There are types and orders of angels who perform specific services in the *cosmic hierarchy.*

The fallen angels are those who followed *Lucifer* in the Great Rebellion and whose consciousness therefore "fell" to lower levels of awareness as they were by law "cast down into the earth" (Rev. 12:9) where they continue to amplify the Luciferian rebellion. They are known as the fallen ones, the sons of Belial, the Luciferians.

Antahkarana. (Sanskrit for internal sense organ.) The web of life. The net of *light* spanning *Spirit* and *Matter* connecting and sensitizing the whole of creation within itself and to the heart of God.

Antichrist. When lower-cased, a person or power antagonistic to the Christ or the *light* in all mankind; when capitalized, the specific personification of *evil,* such as *Lucifer, Satan,* Baal, Beelzebub, Ashtaroth, etc. "Little children, it is the last time: and as ye have heard that Antichrist shall come, even now are there many antichrists; whereby we know that it is the last time." (1 John 2:18)

Archangel. An *angel* who has passed certain advanced initiations qualifying him to preside over lesser angels and bands of angels. Each of the *seven rays* has an archangel who, with his divine complement, an *archeia,* presides over the angels serving on that ray. The archangels and archeiai of the rays are as follows: First ray, Archangel Michael and Faith; second ray, Archangel Jophiel and

Christine; third ray, Archangel Chamuel and Charity; fourth ray, Archangel Gabriel and Hope; fifth ray, Archangel Raphael and Mary; sixth ray, Archangel Uriel and Aurora; seventh ray, Archangel Zadkiel and Holy Amethyst.

Archeia (*pl.* archeiai). Feminine complement and *twin flame* of an *archangel.*

Arhat. (1) A buddhist monk who has attained nirvana. (2) One undergoing the initiations of the Buddha.

Ascended being. *See* Ascended master.

Ascended master. One who has mastered time and space and in the process gained the mastery of the self, balanced at least 51 percent of his *karma,* fulfilled his divine plan, and ascended into the *Presence* of the I AM THAT I AM; one who inhabits the planes of *Spirit,* or heaven.

Ascension. The ritual whereby the soul reunites with the *Spirit,* the *I AM Presence.* The ascension is the final initiation of the soul after its sojourn in time and space. It is the reward of the righteous that is the gift of God after the final judgment in which every man is judged according to his works. (Rev. 20:12) The ascension was demonstrated publicly by Elijah, who ascended "in a chariot of fire," and by Jesus, who ascended from Bethany's hill. It is the goal of life for the *sons and daughters of God.*

Aspirant. One who aspires; specifically, one who aspires to reunion with God through the ritual of the *ascension.* One who aspires to overcome the conditions and limitations of time and space to fulfill the cycles of *karma* and one's reason for being through the *sacred labor.*

Astral. (1) *adj.* Having or carrying the characteristics of the *astral plane.* (2) *n.* A frequency of time and space beyond the physical yet below the mental, corresponding with the *emotional body* of man and the collective subconscious of the race. The term is also used in a negative context to refer to that which is impure or "psychic." *See also* Psychic.

Astral plane. The plane on which the emotions of mankind register collectively. This plane is intended to be used for the amplification of the pure feelings of God; instead it has been polluted with the impure thoughts and feelings of mankind.

Aura. The forcefield of energy surrounding the soul and the *four lower bodies* on which the impressions, thoughts, feelings, words, and actions of the individual are registered. It has been referred to as the L-field, which some scientists say controls the manifestation of the *physical body.*

Bodies of man. The four lower bodies are four sheaths consisting of four distinct frequencies which surround the soul—the physical, emotional, mental, and etheric. They are the modes of the soul in its journey through time and space. The three higher bodies are the *Christ Self,* the *I AM Presence,* and the *Causal Body. See also* Etheric body, Mental body, Emotional body, and Physical body. *See also* Chart of Your Divine Self.

Body elemental. A being of nature (ordinarily invisible and functioning beyond the physical plane) that serves the soul from the moment of its first incarnation in the planes of *Mater* to tend the *physical body.* About three feet high and resembling the individual whom he serves, the body elemental is the unseen friend and guardian of man. *See also* Elementals.

Brothers of the Golden Robe. An order of *ascended* and *unascended being*s dedicated to the flame of wisdom, headed by the Ascended Master *Kuthumi,* with retreats on the etheric plane in *Shigatse* and *Kashmir.*

Carnal mind. The human ego, the human will, and the human intellect; self-awareness without the Christ; the animal nature of man. "The carnal mind is enmity against God." (Rom. 8:7)

Causal Body. The body of First Cause; concentric spheres of *light* and consciousness surrounding the *I AM Presence* in the planes of *Spirit.* These concentric forcefields of electronic energy are available to the soul to work the works of God upon earth. The energies of the Causal Body may be drawn forth through invocation made to the I AM Presence in the name of the Christ. The Causal Body is the dwelling place of the Most High God to which Jesus referred when he said, "In my Father's house are many mansions." (John 14:2) The Causal Body is the mansion or the habitation of the Spirit to which the soul returns through the ritual of the *ascension.* The Causal Body as the star of each man's divine individuality was referred to by Paul when he said, "One star differeth from another star in glory." (1 Cor. 15:41) *See also* Chart of Your Divine Self.

Central sun. *See* Great Central Sun.

Chakra. Sanskrit for wheel, disc, circle. Term used to denote the centers of *light* anchored in the *etheric body* and governing the flow of energy to the four lower *bodies of man.* There are seven major chakras corresponding to the *seven rays,* five minor chakras corresponding to the five secret rays, and a total of 144 light centers in the body

of man. The seven major chakras, their corresponding rays, Sanskrit names, and colors are
as follows: First ray, throat, Vishuddha, blue;
second ray, crown, Sahasrāra, yellow; third ray,
heart, Anāhata, pink; fourth ray, base of the
spine, Mūlādhāra, white; fifth ray, third eye,
Ājnā, green; sixth ray, solar plexus, Manipūra,
purple and gold; seventh ray, seat of the soul,
Svādhishthāna, violet.

Chamuel. *See* Archangel.

Chart of Your Divine Self. (See illustration facing
page 94.) There are three figures represented in the
chart, which we will refer to as the upper figure,
the middle figure, and the lower figure. The upper
figure is the *I AM Presence,* the I AM THAT I AM,
God individualized for every son and daughter
of the Flame. The Divine Monad consists of the
I AM Presence surrounded by the spheres (rings
of color, of *light*) which comprise the *Causal Body.*
This is the body of First Cause that contains
within it man's "treasure laid up in heaven" — perfect works, perfect thoughts and feelings, perfect
words — energies that have ascended from the
plane of action in time and space as the result of
man's correct exercise of free will and his correct
qualification of the stream of life that issues forth
from the heart of the Presence and descends to
the level of the *Christ Self.*

The middle figure in the chart is the mediator
between God and man, called the Christ Self, the
Real Self, or the *Christ consciousness.* It has also
been referred to as the Higher Mental Body. The
Christ Self overshadows the *lower self,* which consists of the soul evolving through the four planes
of *Matter* in the *four lower bodies* corresponding
to the planes of earth, air, fire, and water; that is,

the *etheric body,* the *mental body,* the *emotional body,* the *physical body.*

The three figures of the chart correspond to the Trinity of Father (the upper figure), Son (the middle figure), and Holy Spirit (the lower figure), which the evolving soul is intended to become and for whom the body is the temple. The lower figure is the nonpermanent aspect of being which is made permanent through the ritual of the *ascension.* The ascension is the process whereby the lower figure, having balanced his *karma* and fulfilled his divine plan, merges first with the Christ consciousness and then with the living Presence of the I AM THAT I AM. Once the ascension has taken place, the soul, the corruptible aspect of being, becomes the incorruptible one, a permanent atom in the body of God. The Chart of Your Divine Self is therefore a diagram of yourself—past, present, and future.

The lower figure represents mankind evolving in the planes of Matter. This is how you should visualize yourself standing in the *violet flame,* which you invoke in the name of the I AM Presence and in the name of the Christ in order to purify your four lower bodies in preparation for the ritual of the alchemical marriage—your soul's reunion with the *Spirit,* the I AM Presence. The lower figure is surrounded by a tube of light, which is projected from the heart of the I AM Presence in answer to your call. It is a field of fiery protection sustained in Spirit and in Matter for the sealing of the identity of the overcomer. The *threefold flame* within the heart is the spark of life projected from the I AM Presence through the Christ Self and anchored in the etheric planes in the heart *chakra* for the purpose of the soul's evolution in Matter. Also called the Christ flame, the threefold flame is the spark of man's divinity, his potential for Godhood.

The crystal cord is the stream of light that descends from the heart of the I AM Presence through the Christ Self, thence to the four lower bodies to sustain the soul's vehicles of expression in time and space. It is over this cord that the energy of the Presence flows, entering the being of man at the top of the head and providing the energy for the pulsation of the threefold flame and the physical heartbeat. When a round of the soul's incarnation in Matter-form is complete, the I AM Presence withdraws the crystal cord, the threefold flame returns to the level of the Christ, and the energies of the four lower bodies return to their respective planes.

The dove of the Holy Spirit descending from the heart of the Father is shown just above the head of the Christ. When the individual man, as the lower figure, puts on and becomes the Christ consciousness as Jesus did, the descent of the Holy Spirit takes place and the words of the Father, the I AM Presence, are spoken, "This is my beloved Son in whom I AM well pleased." (Matt. 3:17)

A more detailed explanation of the Chart of Your Divine Self is given in the Keepers of the Flame Lessons and in *Climb the Highest Mountain* by Mark and Elizabeth Prophet, published by The Summit Lighthouse.

Chela. In India, a disciple of a religious teacher (<Hindi *celā* <Skt *ceṭa* slave). A term used generally to refer to a student of the *ascended masters* and their teachings. Specifically, a student of more than ordinary self-discipline and devotion initiated

by an ascended master and serving the cause of the *Great White Brotherhood.*

Cherubim. An order of angelic beings devoted to the expansion and protection of the flame of love. Hence cherubim were the guardians of the east gate (the gate of the *Christ consciousness*) of Eden as well as of the Ark of the Covenant. Throughout the *cosmos,* cherubim are found in manifold aspects of service to God and man.

Chohan. Tibetan for lord or master; a chief. Each of the *seven rays* has a chohan who focuses the *Christ consciousness* of the ray. The names of the chohans of the rays are as follows: First ray, *El Morya;* second ray, Lanto; third ray, Paul the Venetian; fourth ray, Serapis Bey; fifth ray, Hilarion; sixth ray, Nada; seventh ray, Saint Germain.

Christ consciousness. The consciousness or awareness of the self as the Christ; the attainment of a level of consciousness commensurate with that which was realized by Jesus the Christ. The Christ consciousness is the fulfillment within the self of that mind which was in Christ Jesus. It is the attainment of the balanced awareness of *power, wisdom, and love*—of Father, Son, and Holy Spirit—through the balanced manifestation of the *threefold flame* within the heart. *See also* Chart of Your Divine Self.

Christ Self. The individualized focus of "the only begotten of the Father full of grace and truth" (John 1:14); the universal Christ individualized as the true identity of the soul; the *Real Self* of every man, woman, and child to which the soul must rise. The Christ Self is the mediator between a man and his God; it is a man's own personal mentor, priest and prophet, master and teacher. Total identification with the Christ Self defines the Christed one, the Christed being, or the *Christ consciousness. See also* Chart of Your Divine Self.

Color rays. The *light* emanations of the Godhead; e.g., the seven rays of the white light which emerge through the prism of the *Christ consciousness* are (1) blue, (2) yellow, (3) pink, (4) white, (5) green, (6) purple and gold, and (7) violet. There are also five "secret rays" which emerge from the white-fire core of being.

Cosmic consciousness. (1) God's awareness of himself in and as the *cosmos.* (2) Man's awareness of himself in and as God's cosmic self-awareness. The awareness of the self fulfilling the cycles of the cosmos; the awareness of the self as God in cosmic dimensions; the attainment of initiations leading to a cosmic awareness of selfhood.

Cosmic Egg. The spiritual-material universe, including a seemingly endless chain of galaxies, star systems, worlds known and unknown, whose center or white-fire core is called the *Great Central Sun.* The Cosmic Egg has both a spiritual and a material center. Although we discover the Cosmic Egg from the standpoint of our physical senses and perspective, all of the dimensions of *Spirit* can also be known and experienced within the Cosmic Egg. The Cosmic Egg represents the bounds of man's habitation in this cosmic cycle.

Cosmic hierarchy. Beings who have evolved out of God's awareness of his own *cosmic consciousness,* each being personifying an aspect of that consciousness and thereby occupying a specific office in *hierarchy.* Included in the cosmic hierarchy are the Solar Logoi, Elohim, *archangels, ascended* *master*s, elemental and cosmic beings, solar hierarchies, and hierarchs of planetary, interplanetary, and galactic systems.

Cosmic law. That law which governs all manifestation throughout the *cosmos* in the planes of *Spirit* and *Matter.*

Cosmos. The world or universe regarded as an orderly, harmonious system. The material cosmos consists of the entire manifestation in the planes of *Matter* of universes known and unknown. All that exists in time and space comprises the cosmos. There is also a spiritual cosmos, which includes the counterpart of the material cosmos and beyond.

Creator, Preserver, and Destroyer. The Hindu Trinity of Brahma, Vishnu, and Shiva. God the Father is seen as the Creator, God the Son is seen as the Preserver, and God the Holy Spirit is seen as the Destroyer.

Decree. (1) *n.* (a) a foreordaining will, an edict or fiat, a foreordaining of events; (b) a prayer invoking the *light* of God for and on behalf of the evolutions of mankind in the name of the Christ and in the name of the *I AM Presence.* (2) *v.* (a) to decide, to declare, to command or enjoin; to determine or order; to ordain; (b) to invoke the light of God aloud by the power of the spoken word in rhythm and in harmony.

The decree is the most powerful of all applications to the Godhead. It is the command of the *son* or *daughter of God* made in the name of the I AM Presence and the Christ for the will of the Almighty to come into manifestation as above, so below. It is the means whereby the kingdom of God becomes a reality here and now through the power of the spoken word. It may be short or long

and usually is marked by a formal preamble and a
closing, or acceptance.

Discipleship. The state of being an adherent of the
Christ and of the teachings of the *Great White
Brotherhood;* the process of attaining self-mastery
through self-discipline in the initiations of the
Buddha, the World Teachers, and the *ascended
masters*.

Divine Ego. Awareness of true selfhood in and as the
Christ Self or the *I AM Presence;* the *Higher Self*
of man.

Divine Manchild. The Manchild born to the Woman
clothed with the sun (Rev. 12) is the incarnation of
the Christ for the Aquarian Age in the one and the
many *sons and daughters of God* whose destiny it is
to focus the *Christ consciousness* to the evolutions
of earth. Specifically, the term "Manchild" refers
to the child who has the gift of the Holy Spirit from
his mother's womb, e.g., John the Baptist and
Jesus.

Elementals. Beings of earth, air, fire, and water;
nature spirits who are the servants of God and man
in the planes of *Matter* for the establishment and
maintenance of the physical plane as the platform
for the soul's evolution. Elementals who serve the
fire element are called salamanders; those who
serve the air element are called sylphs; those
who serve the water element are called undines;
those who serve the earth element are called
gnomes. (See "God in Nature," chapter 7 of *Climb
the Highest Mountain* by Mark and Elizabeth
Prophet.) *See also* Body elemental.

El Morya Khan, the Ascended Master. Lord (*Chohan*) of the First *Ray* of God's Will, Chief of the

Darjeeling Council of the *Great White Brother-hood,* founder of The Summit Lighthouse, teacher and sponsor of the *Messenger*s Mark and Elizabeth Prophet. El Morya was embodied as the Irish poet Thomas Moore, Akbar the Great, Sir Thomas More, Thomas à Becket, and Melchior, one of the three wise men.

Emotional body. One of the four lower *bodies of man;* the body intended to be the vehicle of the desires and feelings of God made manifest in the being of man. Also called the astral body, the desire body, and the feeling body.

Etheric body. One of the four lower *bodies of man;* called the envelope of the soul, holding the blueprint of the perfect image to be outpictured in the world of form. Also called the memory body.

Evil. *E*nergy-*veil;* the veil of misqualified energy which man imposes upon *Matter* through his misuse of the *sacred fire.*

Four lower bodies. *See* Bodies of man, Physical body, Mental body, Emotional body, and Etheric body.

Gabriel. *See* Archangel.

Goal-fitting. A term used by *El Morya* to describe the fitting of the evolving soul consciousness for the goal of reunion with God; a process of discipline and initiation which souls preparing for the *ascension* undergo under the direction of the *ascended masters.*

God flame. The flame of God; the *sacred fire;* the identity, being, and consciousness of God in and as the white-fire core of being.

God Presence. *See* I AM Presence.

Great Central Sun. The nucleus or white-fire core of the *Cosmic Egg*. (The God Star Sirius is the focus of the Great Central Sun in our sector of the galaxy.)

Great Hub. The center of the *cosmos;* the *Great Central Sun.*

Great White Brotherhood. The fraternity of saints, sages, and *ascended master*s of all ages who, coming from every nation, race, and religion, have reunited with the *Spirit* of the living God and who comprise the heavenly hosts. The term "white" refers to the halo of white *light* that surrounds their forms. The Great White Brotherhood also includes in its ranks certain unascended *chela*s of the ascended masters.

Hierarchy. The chain of individualized beings fulfilling aspects of God's infinite selfhood. Hierarchy is the means whereby God in the *Great Central Sun* steps down the energies of his consciousness, that succeeding evolutions in time and space might come to know the wonder of his love. *See also* Cosmic hierarchy.

Higher Self. The *I AM Presence;* the *Christ Self;* the exalted aspect of selfhood. Used in contrast to *lower self,* or little self, which indicates that which is in a state of becoming whole and attaining the realization of self as God.

Holy Christ Self. *See* Christ Self.

Human consciousness. That consciousness which is aware of the self as human — limited, mortal, subject to error.

Human ego. The point of identity that embraces the *human consciousness* as selfhood.

Human monad. The entire forcefield of self which identifies itself as human. The lower figure in the *Chart of Your Divine Self;* the point of self-awareness out of which all mankind must evolve to the realization of the self as the Christ.

I AM Presence. The I AM THAT I AM (Exod. 3: 13-15); the individualized Presence of God focused for each individual soul. The God-identity of the individual; the Divine Monad; the individual Source. The origin of the soul focused in the planes of *Spirit* just above the physical form; the personification of the *God flame* for the individual. *See also* Chart of Your Divine Self.

Immaculate concept. The pure concept or image of the soul held in the mind of God; any pure thought held by one part of life for and on behalf of another part of life.

Jophiel. *See* Archangel.

Karma. Sanskrit for action or deed. Karma is (1) energy in action; (2) the law of cause and effect and retribution. "Whatsoever a man soweth, that shall he also reap." (Gal. 6:7) Thus the law of karma decrees that from lifetime to lifetime man determines his fate by his actions, including his thoughts, feelings, words, and deeds.

Karmic Lords. *See* Lords of Karma.

Karmic record. The record, written in the Book of Life, in akasha, and in the *etheric body,* of the individual's use of energy since the descent of the soul into the planes of *Mater.* The record of cause-and-effect sequences made by the soul in its interaction with other souls. *See also* Akashic record.

Kashmir. A state in northern India. A retreat of the

Master *Kuthumi* is located in the etheric plane over one of the gardens bordering the lake of Kashmir.

Kuthumi, the Ascended Master. The Master K.H., cofounder (with *El Morya,* known as the Master M.) of the Theosophical movement in 1875 through Helena Petrovna Blavatsky. Head of the order of the *Brothers of the Golden Robe;* serving with Jesus in the office of World Teacher; formerly *Chohan* of the Second Ray. Kuthumi was embodied as Shah Jahan, Saint Francis of Assisi, Balthazar, one of the three wise men, and Pythagoras.

Life record. *See* Karmic record.

Lifestream. The stream of life that comes forth from the one Source, from the *I AM Presence* in the planes of *Spirit,* and descends to the planes of *Matter* where it manifests as the *threefold flame* anchored in the heart *chakra* for the sustainment of the soul in Matter and the nourishment of the four lower bodies. Used to denote souls evolving as individual "lifestreams" and hence synonymous with the term "individual." Denotes the ongoing nature of the individual through its cycles of individualization.

Light. Spiritual light is the energy of God, the potential of the Christ. As the essence of *Spirit,* the term "light" can be used synonymously with the terms "God," "Christ," and *"sacred fire."* It is the emanation of the *Great Central Sun* and the individualized *I AM Presence.*

Little self. *See* Lower self.

Lords of Karma. The beings who make up the Karmic Board: The Goddess of Liberty; the Great Divine

Director; Portia, the Goddess of Justice; the Ascended Lady Master Nada; Pallas Athena, Goddess of Truth; Kwan Yin, Goddess of Mercy; and Cyclopea. These seven *ascended masters* dispense justice to this system of worlds. All souls must pass before the Karmic Board before and after each incarnation on earth. The Karmic Board, acting in consonance with the individual *I AM Presence* and *Christ Self,* determines when the soul has earned the right to be free from the wheel of *karma* and the round of rebirth.

Lower self. The lesser self, or human self (as opposed to the *Christ Self*); identity based on limitation and the laws of mortality. The lower figure in the *Chart of Your Divine Self.*

Lucifer. From the Latin, meaning "light-bearer." One who attained to the rank of *archangel* and fell from grace through ambition, the pride of the ego, and disobedience to the laws of God. The *angels* who followed him are the fallen ones, also called Luciferians or sons of Belial, who have embodied among the children of God. (See the parable of the tares among the wheat, Matt. 13:24-30, 36-43.) *See also* Satan.

Macrocosm. From the Greek, meaning "great world." The larger *cosmos;* the entire warp and woof of creation which we call the *Cosmic Egg.* Also used to contrast man the microcosm, "the little world," against the backdrop of the larger world in which he lives. *See also* Microcosm.

Man. The *man*ifestation of God. Male and female made in the image and likeness of God. Mankind or the human race.

Manchild. *See* Divine Manchild.

Mantra. A mystical formula or invocation; a word or formula, often in Sanskrit, to be recited or sung for the purpose of intensifying the action of the *Spirit* of God in man. A form of prayer consisting of a word or a group of words that is chanted over and over again to magnetize a particular aspect of the Deity or of a being who has actualized that aspect of the Deity.

Mass consciousness. The collective consciousness of humanity.

Mass mind. The collective mind of humanity.

Mater. Latin for "mother." Mater is the *mater*-ialization of the *God flame,* the feminine polarity of the Godhead. The term is used interchangeably with "Matter" to describe the planes of being that conform with the aspect of God as Mother. The soul that descends from the plane of Spirit abides in time and space in Mater for the purpose of its evolution that necessitates the mastery of time and space and of the energies of God through the correct exercise of free will. The four lower *bodies of man,* of a planet, and of systems of worlds occupy and make up the frequencies of Matter. *See also* Spirit.

Matter. *See* Mater.

Mental body. One of the four lower *bodies of man;* the body that is intended to be the vehicle for the mind of God or the Christ mind. "Let this mind be in you which was also in Christ Jesus." (Phil. 2:5) Until quickened, this body, often called the lower mental body, remains the vehicle for the *carnal mind.*

Messenger. One appointed by the *hierarchy* to deliver to mankind the dictations of the *ascended masters* *ex cathedra* in the power of the spoken word. One who is trained by an ascended master to receive by various methods the words, concepts, teachings, and messages of the *Great White Brotherhood.* One who delivers the law, the prophecies, and the dispensations of God for a people and an age.

Michael. *See* Archangel.

Microcosm. From the Greek meaning "small world." (1) The world of the individual, his *four lower bodies,* his *aura,* and the forcefield of his *karma.* (2) The planet. *See also* Macrocosm.

Misqualification (of energy). The "mist" qualification of fallen man and woman; the spawning of *evil,* or the energy *veil,* through the misuse of free will by the evolutions of time and space. The misapplication of God's energy. The use of God's energy to increase hatred instead of love; fear, doubt, and death instead of self-mastery; darkness instead of *light,* etc.

Mortal consciousness. The awareness of the self as mortal, as subject to the laws of mortality, including *sin,* disease, and death.

Occult. That which is hidden. The "occult" mysteries of the *Great White Brotherhood* held in the retreats of the *ascended masters* for thousands of years are currently being brought forth by the ascended masters through their *messengers.*

Path. "The strait and narrow way that leadeth unto life." (Matt. 7:14) The path of initiation whereby the disciple who pursues the *Christ consciousness* overcomes step by step the limitations of selfhood in time and space and attains thereby reunion with reality through the ritual of the *ascension.*

Physical body. The most dense of the four lower

bodies of man, corresponding with the plane of earth; the body that is the vehicle for God's power and the focal point for the crystallization in form of the energies of the *etheric, mental,* and *emotional bodies.*

Power, wisdom, and love. The trinity of the *threefold flame*—power representing the Father, wisdom the Son, and love the Holy Spirit. The balanced manifestation of these God-qualities in and as the flame within the heart is the definition of Christhood.

Presence. *See* I AM Presence.

Psychic. From the word "psyche," meaning soul. The term "psychic" has come to be used synonymously with the term *"astral"* in its negative context and pertains to the penetration and manipulation of energy at the level of the *astral plane,* the probing of dimensions in time and space beyond the physical. According to the *ascended masters,* one who has involved his energies in what is known as the psychic, psychicism, or psychic phenomena is functioning on the lower astral plane and hence foregoes the opportunity to develop his ability to penetrate and manipulate the energies and octaves of *Spirit,* or God.

Raphael. *See* Archangel.

Rays. Beams of *light* or other radiant energy. The light emanations of the Godhead which, when invoked in the name of God or in the name of the Christ, burst forth as a flame in the world of the individual. Rays may be projected through the God consciousness of *ascended* or *unascended beings* as a concentration of energy taking on numerous God-qualities, such as love, truth, wisdom, healing, etc. Through the misuse of God's energy, certain unascended beings may project rays having negative qualities, such as death rays, sleep rays, hypnotic rays, disease rays, etc. *See also* Color rays.

Readings. Probings of past, present, and future and of planes of consciousness beyond the physical. If readings are *psychic,* they may be the readings of the *human consciousness* in all of its aspects. If readings are *ascended-master* readings, they present an accurate assessment of the integration of the *Christ Self* in the four planes of *Matter* and of the *life record* of the individual from the standpoint of the Christ Self, the Book of Life, the Keeper of the Scrolls, and the *Lords of Karma.*

Real Self. The *Christ Self;* the *I AM Presence;* immortal *Spirit* that is the animating principle of all manifestation. *See also* Chart of Your Divine Self.

Recording angel. The *angel* assigned to the soul to record all its actions, words, deeds, feelings, thoughts — in short, its comings and goings in the planes of *Mater.* The recording angel records each day's events and turns them over to the Keeper of the Scrolls, who is the head of the band of angels known as the angels of record and of all recording angels assigned to the lifewaves evolving in time and space.

Sacred fire. God, *light,* life, energy, the I AM THAT I AM. "Our God is a consuming fire." (Heb. 12:29) The sacred fire is the precipitation of the Holy Ghost for the baptism of souls, for purification, for alchemy and transmutation, and for the realization of the sacred ritual of the return to the One.

Sacred labor. That particular calling, livelihood, or profession whereby one establishes his soul's worth both to himself and to his fellowman. One perfects his sacred labor by developing his God-given talents as well as the gifts and graces of the Holy

Spirit and laying these upon the altar of service to humanity. The sacred labor is not only one's contribution to one's community, but it is the means whereby the soul can balance the *threefold flame* and pass the tests of the *seven rays*. It is an indispensable component of the path to reunion with God through the giving of oneself in practical living for God.

Satan. A lieutenant of *Lucifer* and ranking member of the false *hierarchy*. The personification of *evil,* or the energy *veil.* The one who has deified evil and is therefore called the *devil.* Both Lucifer and Satan and their various lieutenants have been referred to as the adversary, the accuser of the brethren, the tempter, the *Antichrist,* the personification of the *carnal mind* of mankind, the serpent, the beast, the dragon, etc. *See also* Lucifer.

Seraphim. Also known as the seraphic hosts. The order of *angels* dedicated to the focusing of the flame of purity and the consciousness of purity in the *Great Central Sun* and throughout the *cosmos* in the planes of *Spirit* and *Matter.* They serve the *ascension* flame and the ascension temple. Serapis Bey, the Hierarch of the Ascension Temple and *Chohan* of the Fourth Ray, was originally of the order of the Seraphim.

Seven rays. *See* Color rays.

Shigatse. A city of Tibet. On the etheric plane over Shigatse, *Kuthumi* maintains a retreat for disciples of Christ and *Brothers of the Golden Robe,* devotees of the flame of wisdom.

Sin. Any departure from *cosmic law* that is the result of the exercise of free will.

Sons and daughters of God. (1) Those who come forth

as the fruit of the divine union of the spirals of Alpha and Omega; those who have the potential to become the Christ. The creation of the Father-Mother God, made in the image and likeness of the Divine Us, identified by the *threefold flame* of life anchored within the heart. (2) On the path the term "sons and daughters of God" denotes a level of initiation and a rank in *hierarchy* that is above those who are called the children of God — children in the sense that they have not passed the initiations of the *sacred fire* that would warrant their being called sons and daughters of God.

Spirit. The masculine polarity of the Godhead; the coordinate of Matter; God as Father, who of necessity includes within the polarity of himself God as Mother and hence is known as the Father-Mother God. The plane of the *I AM Presence,* of perfection; the dwelling place of the *ascended masters* in the Most High God. When lower-cased, as in "spirits," the term is synonymous with discarnates, or disembodied souls. *See also* Mater.

Threefold flame. The flame of the Christ that is the spark of life anchored in the heart *chakra,* or heart center, of the *sons and daughters of God* and the children of God. The sacred trinity of *power, wisdom, and love* that is the manifestation of the *sacred fire. See also* Chart of Your Divine Self.

Tube of light. (See illustration facing page 94.) The white *light* that descends from the heart of the *I AM Presence* in answer to the call of man as a shield of protection for his four lower bodies and his soul evolution. *See also* Chart of Your Divine Self.

Twin flame. The soul's masculine or feminine counterpart conceived out of the same white-fire core, the fiery ovoid of the *I AM Presence.*

Unascended being. One who has not passed through
the ritual of the *ascension.* (1) One abiding in
time and space who has not yet overcome the
limitations of the planes of *Mater* (as opposed to
an *ascended being,* who has ascended into the
Presence of God). (2) One who has overcome all
limitations of Matter yet chooses to remain in time
and space to focus the consciousness of God for
lesser evolutions.

Universal. God, the One, the Divine Whole; energy
that pervades the *cosmos* in the planes of *Spirit*
and *Matter* as the universal presence of the Holy
Spirit.

Uriel. *See* Archangel.

Violet flame. Seventh-ray aspect of the Holy Spirit.
The *sacred fire* that transmutes the cause, effect,
record, and memory of *sin,* or negative *karma.*
Also called the flame of transmutation, of free-
dom, and of forgiveness. (See pp. 295-98 of *Climb
the Highest Mountain* by Mark and Elizabeth
Prophet, published by The Summit Lighthouse.)
See also Chart of Your Divine Self.

Zadkiel. *See* Archangel.

The Master Koot Hoomi 1884

Incarnations of the Ascended Master Kuthumi

THUTMOSE III, pharaoh, prophet, and high priest in the period of the New Kingdom c. 4160 B.C., who expanded the Egyptian kingdom to include most of the Middle East. His most decisive victory was on a battlefield near Mt. Carmel where he led the entire army single file through narrow Megiddo Pass to surprise and defeat an alliance of 330 rebellious Asian princes—a daring maneuver protested by the pharaoh's terrified officers. Thutmose alone was assured of his plan and rode ahead holding aloft the image of Amon-Ra, the Sun God who had promised him the victory.

PYTHAGORAS, Greek philosopher of the sixth century B.C., the "fair-haired Samian" who was regarded as the son of Apollo. As a youth, Pythagoras conferred freely with priests and scholars, eagerly seeking scientific proof of the inner law revealed to him in meditation upon Demeter, the Mother of the Earth. His quest for the great synthesis of truth led him to Palestine, Arabia, India, and finally to the temples of Egypt where he won the confidence of the priests of Memphis and was gradually accepted into the mysteries of Isis at Thebes. When Asian conqueror Cambyses launched a savage invasion of Egypt c. 529 B.C., Pythagoras was exiled to Babylon where the prophet Daniel still served as king's minister. Here rabbis revealed to him the inner teachings of the I AM THAT I AM given to Moses, and here Zoroastrian magi tutored him in music, astronomy, and the sacred science of invocation. After twelve years, Pythagoras left Babylon and founded a brotherhood of initiates at Crotona, a busy Dorian seaport in southern Italy. His "city of the elect" was a mystery school of the Great White Brotherhood where carefully selected men and women pursued a philosophy based upon the mathematical expression of universal law, illustrated in music and in the rhythm and harmony of a highly disciplined way of life. After a five-year probation of strict silence, Pythagorean "mathematicians" progressed through a series of initiations, developing the intuitive faculties of the heart whereby the son or daughter of God may become, as Pythagoras' *Golden Verses* state, "a deathless

God divine, mortal no more." At Crotona, Pythagoras
delivered his lectures from behind a screen in a veiled language which could be fully comprehended only by the most
advanced initiates. The most significant phase of his instruction concerned the fundamental concept that number is both
the form and the essence of creation. He formulated the
essential parts of Euclid's geometry and advanced astro-
nomical ideas which led to Copernicus' hypotheses. It is
recorded that two thousand citizens of Crotona gave up their
customary lifestyle and assembled together in the Pythagorean community under the wise administration of the Council
of Three Hundred — a governmental, scientific, and religious
order who later exercised great political influence throughout Magna Grecia. Pythagoras, the "indefatigable adept,"
was ninety when Cylon, a rejected candidate of the mystery
school, incited a violent persecution. Standing in the court-
yard of Crotona, he read aloud from a secret book of
Pythagoras, *Hieros Logos* (Holy Word), distorting and ridi-
culing the teaching. When Pythagoras and forty of the leading members of the Order were assembled, Cylon set fire to
the building and all but two of the council members were
killed. As a result, the community was destroyed and much
of the original teaching was lost. Nevertheless, "The Master"
has influenced many great philosophers, including Plato,
Aristotle, Augustine, Thomas Aquinas, and Francis Bacon.

BALTHAZAR, one of the three Magi (astronomer/adepts)
who followed the star (the I AM Presence) of the Manchild
born to the Virgin Mary. Believed to have been the King of
Ethiopia, Balthazar brought the treasure of his realm, the
gift of frankincense to Christ, the eternal High Priest.

SAINT FRANCIS OF ASSISI, the divine *poverello*, who
renounced family and wealth and embraced "Lady Poverty,"
living among the poor and the lepers, finding unspeakable
joy in imitating the compassion of Christ. While kneeling at
Mass on the feast of St. Matthias in 1209, he heard the gospel
of Jesus read by the priest and the Lord's command to his
apostles, "Go, preach." Francis left the little church and
immediately began evangelizing, preaching the doctrine of
reincarnation as Jesus had taught and converting many
disciples, including the noble Lady Clare who later left her

home dressed as the bride of Christ and presented herself to Francis for admittance to the mendicant order. One of the many legends surrounding the lives of Francis and Clare describes their meal at Santa Maria degli Angeli where Francis spoke so lovingly of God that all were enraptured in Him. Suddenly the people of the village saw the convent and the woods ablaze and running hastily to quench the flames, they beheld the little company enfolded in brilliant light with arms uplifted to heaven. God revealed to St. Francis the divine presence in "brother sun" and "sister moon" and rewarded his devotion with the stigmata of Christ crucified. The prayer of St. Francis is yet spoken by people of all faiths throughout the world: "Lord, make me an instrument of thy peace!..."

SHAH JAHAN, Mogul emperor of India in the sixteenth century who overthrew the corrupt government of his father Jahangir and restored, in part, the noble ethics of his grandfather Akbar the Great. During his enlightened reign, the splendor of the Mogul court reached its zenith and India entered her golden age of art and architecture. Shah Jahan lavished the imperial treasury not only on music and paintings, but especially on the construction of awesome monuments, mosques, temples, and thrones throughout India, some of which may still be seen today. The famous Taj Mahal, "the miracle of miracles, the final wonder of the world," was built as a tomb for his beloved wife, Mumtaz Mahal, who died in 1631 giving birth to their fourteenth child. Shah Jahan spared no effort in making the temple "as beautiful as she was beautiful." It is the symbol of the Mother principle and the shrine of his eternal love for his twin flame.

ASCENDED MASTER KUTHUMI, formerly Chohan of the Second Ray of Divine Illumination, now serves with Jesus as World Teacher. He is the hierarch of the Cathedral of Nature, in Kashmir, India, and head of the Brothers of the Golden Robe. Kuthumi also maintains a focus at Shigatse, Tibet, where he plays sacred classical music of East and West and compositions of the heavenly hosts as well as of earth's early root races on an organ keyed to the music of the spheres, drawing souls by the sacred sound that is God out of the astral plane into the etheric retreats of the Brotherhood.

THE SEVEN RAYS AND THE SEVEN CHAKRAS

Seven Rays of the Flames Magnetized on the Seven Days of the Week	God-Qualities Amplified through Invocation to the Flame	Chakras, or Centers: Chalices of Light Sustaining the Frequencies of the Seven Rays in the Four Lower Bodies
First Ray Will of God (Blue) Magnified on Tuesday	Omnipotence, perfection, protection, faith, desire to do the will of God through the power of the Father	Throat (Blue)
Second Ray Wisdom of God (Yellow) Magnified on Sunday	Omniscience, understanding, illumination, desire to know God through the mind of the Son	Crown (Yellow)
Third Ray Love of God (Pink) Magnified on Monday	Omnipresence, compassion, charity, desire to be God in action through the love of the Holy Spirit	Heart (Pink)
Fourth Ray Purity of God (White) Magnified on Friday	Purity, wholeness, desire to know and be God through purity of body, mind, and soul through the consciousness of the Divine Mother	Base of the Spine (White)
Fifth Ray Science of God (Green) Magnified on Wednesday	Truth, healing, constancy, desire to precipitate the abundance of God through the immaculate concept of the Holy Virgin	Third Eye (Green)
Sixth Ray Peace of God (Purple and Gold) Magnified on Thursday	Ministration of the Christ, desire to be in the service of God and man through the mastery of the Christ	Solar Plexus (Purple and Gold)
Seventh Ray Freedom of God (Violet) Magnified on Saturday	Freedom, ritual, transmutation, transcendence, desire to make all things new through the application of the laws of Alchemy	Seat of the Soul (Violet)

AND THE BEINGS WHO ENSOUL THEM

Chohans, or Lords, Focusing the Christ Consciousness of the Ray; Location of Their Retreats	Archangels and Divine Complements Focusing the Solar Consciousness of the Ray; Location of Their Retreats	Elohim and Divine Complements Focusing the God Consciousness of the Ray; Location of Their Retreats
El Morya Darjeeling, India	**Michael** **Faith** Banff and Lake Louise, Canada	**Hercules** **Amazonia** Half Dome, Sierra Nevada, California, U.S.A.
Lanto Grand Teton, Teton Range, Wyoming, U.S.A.	**Jophiel** **Christine** South of the Great Wall near Lanchow, North Central China	**Apollo** **Lumina** Western Lower Saxony, Germany
Paul the Venetian Southern France	**Chamuel** **Charity** St. Louis, Missouri, U.S.A.	**Heros** **Amora** Lake Winnipeg, Canada
Serapis Bey Luxor, Egypt	**Gabriel** **Hope** Between Sacramento and Mount Shasta, California, U.S.A.	**Purity** **Astrea** Near Gulf of Archangel, southeast arm of White Sea, Russia
Hilarion Crete, Greece	**Raphael** **Mother Mary** Fatima, Portugal	**Cyclopea** **Virginia** Altai Range where China, Siberia, and Mongolia meet, near Tabun Bogdo
Nada Saudi Arabia	**Uriel** **Aurora** Tatra Mountains south of Cracow, Poland	**Peace** **Aloha** Hawaiian Islands
Saint Germain Transylvania, Romania Table Mountain in Teton Range, Wyoming, U.S.A.	**Zadkiel** **Amethyst** Cuba	**Arcturus** **Victoria** Near Luanda, Angola, Africa

Index of Scripture

Index

Abandon, delirious, 61

Ability: to fathom other planes of existence, 12; to read the human aura, 41. *See also* Capacities; Talents

Abortion, of the divine intent, 34

Absolute, penetration of the, 82

Abundance, 82; of the green light, 36; "...and he shall have more abundance...," 25. *See also* Treasure(s); Wealth

Abundant life, 32, 66, 81; opportunity for the, 8; self-realization through the, 11

Acceptance, of a decree, 106

Accuser of the brethren, 116. *See also* Fallen ones

Act(s), 43; of mercy, chap. X n.6; that which is not immaculate in someone's, 37. *See also* Action(s)

Action(s): an angel assigned to record all, 115; arena of, 15; cast into the discard pile, 78; divine love in, 36; energies that have ascended from the plane of, 100; energy in, 109; the forcefield on which, are registered, 98; the genius that illumines, 11; karma as Sanskrit for, 109; man determines his fate by his, 109; the Real Self in, 61; responsibility for, 87. *See also* Act(s); Deed(s); Doings; Effort(s); Work(s)

Adam, consciousness partaken of by, 30

Adept(s), 41, 43, 120; defined, 95; "indefatigable adept," 120. *See also* Adeptship; Master(s)

Adeptship, 46, 90. *See also* Adept(s); Attainment; Mastery

Adherent: of the Christ, 106; of the sacred fire, 90. *See also* Devotee(s)

Adjustments, life will make her, 87

Admiration, of every ascended master, 40

Adults, fear to be thought child-like, 52

Advancement, 54, 64; of the soul, 87. *See also* Progress

Adversary, 116, *see* reverse side of *plate* 2. *See also* Enemy

Advice, timeless, 74. *See also* Guidance

Affinity, magnetic, of the aura, 22

Affirmation, of dominion, 77

Afterlife, mysteries of the, 9

Age(s), 58, 59; the seventh, *see* reverse side of *plate* 2; teachers who come in every, 15-16. *See also* Aquarian Age; Era(s); Golden age; Piscean Age

Aim, of the master, 6. *See also* Purpose(s)

Air, 69, 100-101; beings of, 106. *See also* Elemental(s); Elemental beings

Aircraft, 27, 35

Airport traffic controller, 27

Ājnā, 100

Akasha, 109. *See also* Akashic records; Impressions; Record(s)

Akashic records, 25; defined, chap. I n.5, 95. *See also* Akasha; Record(s)

Akbar the Great, 121; El Morya was embodied as, 107

Alchemical marriage, 101. *See also* Bride; Reunion

Alchemist, Great, *plate* 3. *See also* Alchemy

Alchemy, 115; the laws of, 20. *See also* Alchemist

Alliance, with the forces of heaven, 65

Almighty, 45; the will of the, 105. *See also* God

Alpha and Omega, the union of, 117

Altar(s): to false gods, 77; greatness that must be sacrificed upon the,

cosmos, 118; those who have mis-qualified the bulk of their, 86; a tightened spring of, 86; the veil of misqualified, 107; from whence cometh, 49

Energy veil, 113; *see* reverse side of *plate* 2; a personification of the, 116

Enlightened ones, the word of, 9

Enlightenment: a fraternity dedi-cated to, 20; of the race, 62; through self-knowledge, 8; self-realization through, 11. *See also* Illumination; Intelligence; Know-ing; Knowledge; Understanding; Wisdom

Enmity, "The carnal mind is enmity against God," 99

Enoch, 9, 11

Enthusiasm, Kuthumi's, 76

Entrapment, psychic, 66. *See also* Quicksands

Envelope: of flesh and blood, 45; of invulnerability, 65; of the soul, 107. *See also* Sheath

Environment, 46, 52; being weight-ed down by, 42

Equilibrium, disturbing the, of life-streams, 64

Era(s): of holy innocence, 89; of possibility, 49; thoughts from other, 29. *See also* Age(s)

Error(s), 63, 108; acknowledgement that you have made an, 75; free-dom from past, 88; shouting from the housetops of a man's, 75; those who dwell in, 87; in thought, 52. *See also* Sin(s)

Essence: of Christ, *see* reverse side of *plate* 2; of creation, 120; of Spirit, 110; of unseen worlds, 9

Estate, archangels in their God-, 72. *See also* Heaven

Esteem, of the immaculate concept, 81

Eternity, miracle of, 58. *See also* Endlessness; Forever; Immortal-ity; Infinity

Ethereal, shades in the aura which are, 36

Etheric body, 98, 101; centers of light anchored in the, 99; crys-tallization of the energies of the, 114; defined, 107; the record written in the, 109. *See also* Four lower bodies

Etheric plane(s): retreat(s) on the, 99, 109-110, 116; the threefold flame anchored in the, 101. *See also* Plane(s)

Ethics, noble, 121. *See also* Ideals; Standard(s)

Ethiopia, the king of, 120

Euclid's geometry, 120

Eve, consciousness partaken of by, 30

Events: are recorded, 25; a foreor-daining of, 105; not all, are be-nign, 26; the recording angel records each day's, 115. *See also* Condition(s)

Evidence, conclusive, 87. *See also* Proof

Evil: consciousness of good and, 30; defined, 107; deified, as the dev-il, 116; personification of, 96, 116, *see* reverse side of *plate* 2; the spawning of, 113; suppres-sing, 75. *See also* Darkness

Evil One, referred to in the scrip-tures, *see* reverse side of *plate* 2. *See also* Fallen ones

Evolution, 112; the platform for the soul's, 106. *See also* Progress

Ex cathedra, 112-13

Example(s): is the best teacher, 23; of misqualification, 35; of the teacher, 13. *See also* Exemplar; Footsteps

Exemplar, Great, *plate* 2. *See also* Example(s)

Exercise, 54; for the strengthening of the aura, 51-52, 65; a three-fold, 5. *See also* Meditation(s)

Existence: ability to fathom other planes of, 12; challenges of an-other, 9; man endows his deeds with an, 30; a self-centered, 82. *See also* Being; Life

Expansion, of the auric light, 84

Expectancy, of life, 84

Experience(s): crucible of, 87;

Interplanetary systems, hierarchs of, 105
Interpolation: of auras, 77; of auric emanations, 37
Interpretation, of the law or the scriptures, *see* reverse side of *plate* 3
Intuitive faculties, 9, 119
Invasion: of Egypt, 119; of the mind and heart, 81. *See also* Attack
Invincibility, of the King of Kings, 36. *See also* Protection
Invitation: 70; to be of service, 72
Invocation: assistance through, 66; energies drawn forth through, 99; a mantra as an, 112; Pythagoras tutored in the science of, 119; the storing-up of God's light through, 65. *See also* Call(s)
Isis, the mysteries of, 119
Israel: the children of, 12; the lost sheep of the house of, *see* reverse side of *plate* 2; promise given to the prophet of, 10; the Twelve Tribes of, *see* reverse side of *plate* 3
Italy, Crotona in, 119

Jahangir, 121
Jealousy, 27; chartreuse green of, 38
Jesus, *illus., plate* 2, 13, 17, 21, 24, 26, *see* reverse sides of *plates* 2 and 3; consciousness realized by, 103; demonstrated the ascension publicly, 97; the doctrine of reincarnation as, had taught, 120; guarded the ark of the covenant, 9; as the Manchild, 106; mankind will behold, 15; men think that only, ascended, 46; as the messenger for the Christ, 13; Pilate could find no fault with, 42; the portrait of, *see* reverse side of *plate* 3; a promise of, 32; the Prophets received training from, 14; put on and became the Christ consciousness, 102; serves under Lord Maitreya, 18; understanding that, imparted, 60; we have identified the light *as,* 11;

the words of, 89; as World Teacher, 110, 121. *See also* Christ; Master(s)
Jew, *see* reverse side of *plate* 2. *See also* Christ; Israel
Joan of Arc, 77
John, 13, 16, *see* reverse side of *plate* 2. *See also* John the Beloved; John the Revelator
John the Baptist, 15; as the Manchild, 106; as the messenger for Jesus, 13; we have identified the light *as,* 11
John the Beloved, the light that, beheld in the Saviour, 11. *See also* John
John the Revelator, the prophecy given to, 15. *See also* John
Jophiel, Archangel, as the archangel of the second ray, 96. *See also* Archangel(s)
Journey(s): through the portals of life and death, 58; through time and space, 98
Joy(s): 72; of the angels, 39; born in the soul, 87; cup of, 61; eternal, 60; of God, 67; in imitating the compassion of Christ, 120; "...over one sinner that repenteth...," 76; purification of the aura brings, unto the angels, 76; those who cut themselves off from, 70; thoughts of, 30; the trumpet of cosmic, 71. *See also* Cheer; Delight(s)
Judea, preaching in the wilderness of, 13
Judges, of beauty, 40
Judgment: all things ought to go to God for, 75; the gift of God after the final, 97; passing, upon the lives of others, 87; the Pilate of some man's, 66. *See also* Judgments
Judgments, 89. *See also* Judgment
Justice: angels intensify feelings of, 95; ascended masters who dispense, 111
Justice, Goddess of, 111
Justification, violet black of self-righteous, 38

concentrated focus of, 12; the conflagration of the, 78; the correct use of the, 20; defined, 115; each adherent of the, 90; the God flame as the, 107; initiates of the, 18; light as synonymous with, 110; manifestation of the, 117; that transmutes sin, 118; the ultimate tests of the, 17. *See also* Fire

Sacred labor, 97; defined, 115-16. *See also* Calling

Sacrifice, 59; Kuthumi on, 24; no, too great, 82-83; of Saint Germain, *see* reverse side of *plate* 3. *See also* Offering

Sage(s): a fraternity of, 108; Kuthumi in the role of, 18. *See also* Teacher(s)

Sahasrāra, 100

Sailors, 21

Saint Germain: *illus., plate* 3, *see* reverse sides of *plates* 2 and 3; as the chohan of the seventh ray, 103; the Prophets received training from, 14. *See also* Chohan(s)

Saints: faith once delivered unto the, 57; a fraternity of, 108; invoke the angels, 71; thoughts created in the hearts of the, 30. *See also* Ascended master(s)

Salamanders, serve the fire element, 106. *See also* Elemental(s)

Salvation, *see* reverse sides of *plates* 2 and 3. *See also* Redemption

Samuel, the prophet, *see* reverse side of *plate* 2

Sanat Kumara. *See* Ancient of Days

Sanhedrin, 43

Sanskrit: for action or deed, 109; for internal sense organ, 96; a mantra often in, 112; Sanskrit names for the chakras, 100; for wheel, disc, circle, 99

Santa Maria degli Angeli, 121

Satan, 96, 116; the carnal mind personified in, 17; conspirators of, 59; "Get thee behind me, Satan!" 66; "Get thee hence, Satan...," 18; referred to in the scriptures, *see* reverse side of *plate* 2. *See also* Lucifer

Satisfaction, in perceiving the wrongs of others, 23

Saviour, *see* reverse side of *plate* 3; the light that John the Beloved beheld in the, 11; World, *plate* 2. *See also* Christ

Scepticism, rocks of modern, 21

Scholars, Pythagoras conferred with, 119

Schoolroom, this planet as a, 53

Schools. *See* Education; Mystery school(s); University

Science, 5; of partaking of unseen worlds, 9; of perfecting the aura, 5, 26; Pythagoras tutored in the, of invocation, 119; reading the human aura is no ordinary, 22; of religion, *see* reverse side of *plate* 3; and religion wed, 6; of self-knowledge, 8; of the soul, 20; of the spoken Word, *see* reverse side of *plate* 2; of Transmutation, *plate* 3. *See also* Scientific order; Scientists

Scientific order, 120. *See also* Science

Scientists, 5, 98; destiny that has inspired, 8; inspired with wisdom, 19. *See also* Science

Screen, of life, 30

Scriptures, 40; distortions of the, 24; *energy veil* referred to in the, *see* reverse side of *plate* 2; private interpretation of the, *see* reverse side of *plate* 3; which the devil quoted to Jesus, 17. *See also* Biblical centrum; Gospel; Parable; Psalmist; Revelation(s)

Sea: the aura need never be a muddied, 62; of light, 83

Seal: of approval, 41; of God's authority, 71

Seamless garment, 42. *See also* Garment(s)

Seat, of malleability, 83

Seat of the soul, as a chakra, 100. *See also* Chakra(s)

Second Coming, of Christ, 15

Second ray: the archangel and archeia of the, 96-97; the chohan of the, 103; corresponds to the

their, 41; those who have re-united with the, 108. *See also* Holy Spirit; Spirits

Spirits, 117; great, 77. *See also* Figures; Spirit

Spiritual exercise. *See* Exercise

Spirituality, 36, 47, 67. *See also* Devotion(s)

Sponsor: of America, *plate* 3, *see* reverse side of *plate* 3; of the messengers, 107, *see* reverse side of *plate* 3

Spring, a tightened, of energy, 86

Stages, of mastering negative energy, 64

Standard(s), 8, 43. *See also* Ethics

Star(s): of divine radiance, 43; of each man's individuality, 99; God Star, 108; of hope, 59; hope for all beneath, 59; the human aura as a, 83; of the I AM Presence, 120; of the man who becomes one with God, 84; "One star differeth from another star in glory," 99; one, differs from another, in glory, 81; pathway to the, 60; a seemingly endless chain of, systems, 104; of varying intensity, 83. *See also* Galactic systems; Galaxies; Galaxy; Nova; Venus

State(s): of becoming whole, 11; heads of, 15; indulgence in negative, 38

Stigmata, 121

Stone(s): command "these stones be made bread," 17; "...lest... thou dash thy foot against a stone," 17; the temptation to command, be made bread, 58. *See also* Rock(s)

Storehouse, of memory, 25

Strata, protective, of energy, 66

Stream(s): crystal flowing, 6, 85, 88; of immortal perfection, 62; of life, 100, 110; of light from the I AM Presence, 102; of mankind's consciousness, 34; a putrid, 86; of the substance of life, 85. *See also* River

Strength, 46; a fiat of, 23; of God,

70; to perceive a truth, 24; sapping man's, 54. *See also* Firmness; Forte; Fortitude; Strengthening

Strengthening, of your aura and life, 75

Strife, 66. *See also* Discord

Striving, 41. *See also* Aspiration(s)

Struggle: lessening the, 83; the sense of, 57

Student(s), 25; approach studies with the right attitude, 30; of the ascended masters, 102; contact with each, of this course, 6; energizing the consciousness of, 55; the life of each, 51; of the occult, 41; the sincere, 27; at Summit University, 19. *See also* Devotee(s)

Studies: auric, 24; offered at the ascended masters' university, 19

Studies of the Human Aura, 20, 25, 27; Kuthumi's intent in the first two releases of, 32; understanding that Kuthumi seeks to promote in, 60. *See also* Auric studies; Study

Study: of auric emanations, 23; in individual development, 80; of wisdom, 31. *See also* Research; Studies; *Studies of the Human Aura*

Subconscious, collective, of the race, 98. *See also* Mind; Subconscious levels

Subconscious levels: auric contamination may reach, 38; observations transmitted to, 25. *See also* Subconscious

Subjects, hidden from the average seeker, 23

Sublime, the ridiculous detracting from the, 81

Sublimity, of God, 81

Substance, 70; impure, 86; known as akasha, chap. I n.5; of life, 85; nodules of dark and shadowed, 54; overlaid upon the natural vibration, 38; a patine of, 30; thought is made up of, 57. *See also* Dross

Subtleties, negative, 81

Witness, of Jesus' perfection, 42

Witnesses: the cloud of, 46, 57; as the two candlesticks, 16. *See also* Messenger(s); Two witnesses

Woman: Jesus as the messenger for the Christ in every, 13; the Man-child born to the, 106; the still small voice speaks to every, 11; who will speak the living Word, 36; the Word made flesh in every, 15. *See also* Female; Women

Womb, the child who has the Holy Spirit from his mother's, 106

Women, who will seize the torch of knowledge, 21. *See also* Woman

Wonder: an expression of heaven's, 58; of thyself, 84; of the world, 121. *See also* Miracle

Word, 60, *see* reverse side of *plate* 2; ancient wisdom in the spoken and written, 14; of the enlightened ones, 9; "...every word that proceedeth out of the mouth of God," 17, 59; if God would speak the, 53; incarnate, *plate* 2, *see* reverse side of *plate* 3; the ineffable, 9; the man or woman who will speak the living, 36; the power of the spoken, 5, 105, 113; of the teacher, 13; as the true messenger, 13; the, made flesh, 11; "the Word was made flesh...," 13. *See also* Call(s); Christ

Words: an angel assigned to record, 115; chanted over and over again, 112; forcefield on which, are registered, 98; of the Great White Brotherhood, 113; of the I AM Presence, 102; of Jesus, 26, 60, 89; man determines his fate by his, 109; of the Master, 59; "...but my words shall not pass away," 21; perfect, 100; of the Psalmist, 58; to recite with humility and devotion, 51; the thoughts of those who carelessly read Kuthumi's, 48

Work(s): begun by the Master K.H., 20; every man judged according to his, 97; "Greater works shall ye do...," 32; perfect, 100;

"...that they may see your good works...," 60; when God does his perfect, 59; working the, of God upon earth, 99. *See also* Action(s); Service(s)

Workers, the shuttle of cosmic, 63. *See also* Helpers

World, 58; "The children of this world are in their generation wiser...," 32; the cosmic temple of the, 78; distractions of the, 81; envisioning a better, 8; external and internal, 25; few have probed beyond the finite, 13; the flow of perfection into your, 61; the gloom of the, 90; has its conspiracies, 59; how to live in this, 8; how to prepare for the, to come, 8-9; influences of the, 29; in its transitory period, 21; the kingdoms of the, 18; knowledge in the marts of the, 21; larger, 111; the light of the, 48; the light which lighteth every man that cometh into the, 11-12; loving the things of the, 81; manifestation of reality in your, 33; the master of one's, 6, 54; microcosm meaning "small world," 113; molding the whole, in the divine image, 55-56; probing the known and unknown, 6; redemption of the, 63; regarded as an orderly system, 105; a wonderful, 76. *See also* Earth; Planet

World Mother, the one who serves directly under the, 19

World Teacher(s), 21, *plate* 2; have come to the fore, 20; have sponsored education, 19; initiations of the, 106; Jesus and Kuthumi in the office of, 18, 110; Kuthumi serves as, 121. *See also* Teacher(s)

Worldly-wise, 52. *See also* Worldly-wise spirit

Worldly-wise spirit, 70. *See also* Worldly-wise

Worlds: ascended masters who dispense justice to this system of, 111; the four lower bodies of systems of, 112; a messenger of far-

For information on The Summit Lighthouse, Church Universal and Triumphant, Summit University, Montessori International, conferences and seminars conducted by Elizabeth Clare Prophet, Summit Lighthouse study groups closest to you, free literature, and current Pearls of Wisdom sent weekly, write Camelot, Box A, Malibu, CA 90265, or call (213) 880-5300. Our International Headquarters is located at Camelot, 26800 West Mulholland Highway (corner of Mulholland Highway and Las Virgenes Road), Calabasas, CA 91302. Or contact any of the following Community Teaching Centers:

Los Angeles
Ashram of the World Mother
1130 Arlington Avenue
Los Angeles, CA 90019
(213) 732-0171

Santa Barbara
Keepers of the Flame Motherhouse
2112 Santa Barbara Street
Santa Barbara, CA 93105
(805) 682-7631

San Francisco
2109 Fourteenth Avenue
San Francisco, CA 94116
(415) 564-6433

Colorado Springs
Retreat of the Resurrection Spiral
First and Broadmoor
Colorado Springs, CO 80906
(303) 475-2133

Minneapolis/St. Paul
Hiawatha House
1206 Fifth Street SE
Minneapolis, MN 55414
(612) 331-6960

Chicago
4247-49 N. Hazel Street
Chicago, IL 60613
(312) 477-8980

Detroit
23647 Woodward Avenue
Pleasant Ridge, MI 48069
(313) 545-6769
(313) 652-4375

Washington, D.C.
Rakoczy Mansion
4715 Sixteenth Street NW
Washington, D.C. 20011
(202) 882-1900

Philadelphia
Box A
Bryn Mawr, PA 19010
(215) 353-0531

Vancouver
2515 Cornwall Avenue
Vancouver, B.C.
Canada V6K 1C1
(604) 738-9195

Summit University®

A COLLEGE OF RELIGION, CULTURE, AND SCIENCE
OF CHURCH UNIVERSAL AND TRIUMPHANT

In every age there have been some, the few, who have pursued an understanding of God and of selfhood that transcends the current traditions of doctrine and dogma. Compelled by a faith that knows the freedom of love, they have sought to expand their awareness of God by probing and proving the infinite expressions of his law. Through the true science of religion, they have penetrated the 'mysteries' of both Spirit and Matter and come to experience God as the All-in-all.

Having discovered the key to reality, these sons and daughters of God have drawn about them disciples who would pursue the disciplines of the law of the universe and the inner teachings of the 'mystery schools'. Thus Jesus chose his apostles, Bodhidharma his monks, and Pythagoras his initiates at Crotona, Gautama Buddha called his disciples to form the *sangha* (community), and King Arthur summoned his knights to the quest for the Holy Grail at the Table Round.

Summit University is a mystery school for men and women of the twentieth century who would pursue the great synthesis of the teachings of the ascended masters — the few who have overcome in every age, the many who now stand as our elder brothers and sisters on the Path. Together Gautama Buddha and Lord Maitreya sponsor Summit University with the World Teachers Jesus and Kuthumi, El Morya, Lanello, and Saint Germain, Confucius, Mother Mary, Moses and Mohammed, the Archangels Michael and Gabriel, and "numberless numbers" of "saints robed in white" — the Great 'White' Brotherhood. To this university of the Spirit they lend their flame, their counsel, the momentum of their attainment, and the living teaching for us who would follow in their footsteps to the source of that reality they have become.

Founded in 1971 under the direction of the Messengers Mark L. Prophet and Elizabeth Clare Prophet, Summit University currently holds three twelve-week retreats each year — fall, winter, and spring quarters — as well as five two-week summer retreats and healing weekend retreats. All of the courses are based on the unfoldment of the inner potential of the Christ, the Buddha, and the Mother. Through the teachings of the ascended masters given through their messengers, students at Summit University pursue the disciplines on the path of the ascension for the soul's ultimate reunion with the Spirit of the living God.

This includes the study of the sacred scriptures of East and West taught by Jesus and Gautama; exercises in the self-mastery of the energies of the chakras and the aura under Kuthumi and Djwal Kul; beginning and intermediate studies in alchemy under the Ascended Master Saint Germain; the Cosmic Clock — a new-age astrology for charting the cycles of karma and dharma given by Mother Mary; the science of the spoken Word in conjunction with prayer, meditation, and visualization — the key to soul liberation in the Aquarian age; weekly healing services, "Be Thou Made Whole!" at the Ashram of the World Mother and the Chapel of the Holy Grail at Camelot in which the messenger gives personal and planetary healing invocations; the psychology of the family, the marriage ritual and meditations for the conception of new-age children; counseling for community service through the sacred labor; the teachings and meditations of the Buddha taught by Gautama Buddha, Lord Maitreya, Lanello, and the five Dhyani Buddhas; and individual initiations transferred to each student from the ascended masters through the messengers.

Summit University is a twelve-week spiral that begins with you as self-awareness and ends with you as God Self-awareness. As you traverse the spiral, light intensifies, darkness is transmuted. You experience the rebirth day by day as the old man is put off and the new man is put on. Energies are aligned, chakras are cleared, and the soul is poised for the victorious fulfillment of the individual divine plan.

In addition to preparing the student to enter into the Guru-chela relationship with the ascended masters and the path of initiation outlined in their retreats, the academic standards of Summit University, with emphasis on the basic skills of both oral and written communication, prepare students to enroll in top-level undergraduate and graduate programs and to become efficient members of the national and international community. A high school diploma (or its equivalent) is required and a willingness to become the disciplined one — the disciple of the Great God Self of all.

Summit University is a way of life that is an integral part of Camelot — an Aquarian-age community secluded on a beautiful 218-acre campus in the Santa Monica Mountains west of Los Angeles near the beaches of Malibu. Here ancient truths become the law of everyday living to hundreds of kindred souls brought together again for the fulfillment of the mission of the Christ through the oneness of the Holy Spirit.

For information write or call Summit University, Box A, Malibu, CA 90265   (213) 880-5300.